MW00343671

HOW TO WRITE A
SUCCESSFUL SERIES

HOW TO WRITE A SUCCESSFUL SERIES

Writing Strategies for Authors

HELEN B. SCHEUERER

First printing, 2022

Print paperback ISBN 978-0-6452216-7-1

Print hardcover ISBN 978-0-6452216-8-8

Ebook ISBN 978-0-6452216-9-5

Cover design by Miblart

Contents

A note on spelling   ix
Introduction   xi

Section I: Understanding Book Series   1

1. The Basics of Writing a Series   3
2. Why Write in a Series?   7
3. The Resistance to Writing a Series   14

Section II: Series Preparation   21

4. Write What You Love   23
5. Do Your Research   29
6. Planning Your Series   44
7. Outlining Your Series   56
8. Approaching a Series as a Discovery Writer   72

Section III: Writing Your Series and Must-Have Elements   81

9. It All Starts with Book One   83
10. Keep a Series Bible   91
11. Craft a Compelling Cast of Characters   103
12. Use Foreshadowing and Breadcrumbs   113
13. Use Open Loops and Cliffhangers   122
14. Write Nail-Biting Sequels and Later Books   132
15. Exit and Expansion Strategies Within a Series   140
16. Writing a Killer Series Ending   145

Section IV: Long-Term Strategies for Writing Series   155

17. Write Longer Series   157
18. Your Second Series and Beyond   162
19. The Power of the Reader Magnet   166
20. Create a Flagship or Anchor Series   176

Section V: Leveraging Literary Universes, Same-World and Second-Generation Series   183

21. What are Literary Universes, Same-World and   185
    Second-Gen Series?
22. Why Use the Same World?   190
23. How to Lead Your Readers from Series to Series   193
    in Your Literary Universe

Section VI: All the Rest   199

24. Combating Series Fatigue   201
25. Managing Multiple Books and Multiple Series   206
26. Mistakes Made and Lessons Learned   214
27. Commonly Asked Questions About Writing a   221
    Series

Conclusion   233
References   235
Recommended Resources   243
Bonuses   247
Acknowledgements   249
About the Author   251
By the Same Author   253

For Sacha Black

A note on spelling

Australian/British spellings have been used throughout this book,
unless material is directly quoted.

Introduction

"Remember to revel in the creative joy of the process. This is my dream job. I'm doing the thing I've wanted to do since I was seven years old…"
(Helen Scheuerer, Author Diaries, August 25th, 2021)

All authors dream of their own version of success: perhaps it's making a living from their writing; or resonating with their readers; or receiving rave reviews… I have done all of these things and more by writing in a series, and in this book, I'll show you exactly how.

In 2017, I published my debut novel, *Heart of Mist*, the first book in a trilogy called *The Oremere Chronicles*. I published its sequels, *Reign of Mist* and *War of Mist*, in the two years that followed, and experienced a level of success I had not anticipated. In under three years, just three books in a series generated well over a quarter of a million dollars (AUD) in revenue. That's not including audiobook royalties, the sales that followed in the more recent years, or the royalties from associated products like the prequel collection, *Dawn of Mist*, or the omnibus. I learned the power of writing in series from day one, and over the course of this book, you will too.

Series are the bread and butter of the fantasy genre, and so when I started down the young adult (YA) fantasy road with that first book, I fell into writing series quite naturally and without much forethought. Growing up, I always loved the form – I read almost exclusively in series: *Deltora Quest, Harry Potter, Redwall, A Series of Unfortunate Events, The Hunger Games, Artemis Fowl...* I devoured them, experiencing the thrill, the addiction and the joys of the structure firsthand. So it was only natural that when it came to writing my own books, committing to a series was a simple decision. But did I understand what it was about this form that had me in its thrall? Not quite.

Back then, besides the knowledge that a good series could provide weeks, months or even years of entertainment and joy, I had no *real* understanding as to why series seemed to be the common denominator for authors who maintained long-term success, despite the fact that I myself had experienced that very thing. I was able to quit my job after only five months of being a published author and that first trilogy supported me for the next three years, before I started publishing my next series.

In fact, it wasn't until I was over four years into writing full-time that I started to look at writing a series from a more strategic, long-term point of view. I knew if I wanted this dream career to last, my decisions needed to become a lot more informed and a lot more deliberate. My goal was to continue to grow in all areas: my skills in the craft, my readership and, of course, my sales and income. It was this goal that kept bringing me back to the concept of series, and I began to uncover the complex layers of the form, as well as the clever tactics the best authors employed.

Why this book?

For a long while, the idea of writing a book about independent publishing stuck with me. The tidbits of advice I was offering online seemed to be increasingly popular and I regularly received detailed questions via private messages or emails. However, the topic is so broad, and there are so many wonderful books already available, that I struggled with what I wanted to say. That was until a good friend of mine asked me, "What do you want to learn?" Of all my notes and research, I kept coming back to the subject of writing series and how some of the most successful authors I knew were using them in an incredibly strategic way, not only at the publishing level, but before that: at the creation and writing levels. There were techniques authors employed that readers didn't necessarily notice, but that sucked them into an entire catalogue of books. This fascinated me to no end.

I realised I was captivated by the "long game" nature of writing a series or multiple series – how this decision could affect an author's career not just at the time of publication, but in the years to come. So I honed in on the concept of series, I interrogated what had worked for me over the years, and I studied the strategies I saw other authors using that had impacted their careers. The immense worldbuilding, the subtle foreshadowing and the creation of entire literary universes were just the tip of the iceberg.

This book has gone through many different versions to become the one you hold in your hands. The final result is an offering of everything I've learned about writing and using series throughout an indie author career, mostly involving the pre-publication stage. It's about how to craft the strongest foundation for your series to set you up for long-term success.

Why me?

At the time of writing, every book I've published so far has hit #1 on Amazon in various categories within 24 hours, in the US, the UK and Australia. Across various platforms, my series have garnered thousands of reviews, most with an average 4.5-star rating (out of five). With the help of my agent, I have also sold the audio rights for *The Oremere Chronicles* to Audible and my second series, *Curse of the Cyren Queen*, to Podium.

For those into academics, I also hold a Bachelor of Creative Arts majoring in Creative Writing from the University of Wollongong and a Master of Publishing from the University of Sydney (both in Australia). I graduated from both degrees with Distinction. Though I will say this: while I value both degrees immensely, my practical experience out in the indie world will be far more beneficial to you than those pieces of paper.

In other words... I've learned a lot about writing a series since I first started, and I want to share that knowledge with you.

What to expect from this book

This book won't teach you how to publish and market a series – that's a whole other book in itself. This book won't teach you how to become a full-time indie author, nor will it be a silver bullet to bestseller status. While this book includes various techniques for writing a series, at its core are strategies for forging powerful indie author careers and long-term success.

So, let me tell you what this book *is* about... It's about understanding series writing on a deeply strategic level. It's about identifying what to weave through your stories from the get-go to instil that addiction within your reader, that tendency to binge-read – to ensure they surge from one book to the next to the next. It's about aiming high and expanding your catalogue in the most productive and profitable way. It's about familiarising yourself with the challenges of writing in this structure and fighting through the muck. It's about writing intelligently and lucratively. Most of all, this book is about leveraging all this incredible knowledge for long-term success as an indie author.

Who is this book for?

This book is for any indie author who has written, is writing or is thinking about writing a series (or more than one). It's for authors who want to get the most out of the form, both in terms of creating the best possible story and building their career to sustain them long term. This book is specifically for indies who are serious about making a living from their fiction writing and who want to be more strategic in their plans.

What do you mean by "long term"?

I realise this can mean different things to different people, but in the context of this book, let's assume that long term means "for the foreseeable future" or "until retirement". It means a career that can span upwards of a decade, or the career that spans the majority of your adult life.

A note on examples of fiction series

Throughout this book, I'll be referencing a number of well-known fiction series across a range of mediums: books, film and TV. The reason for using multiple mediums is that there is more chance the examples will be universally recognised.

My personal writing and publishing experience is in the fantasy genre; however, I've included other examples to factor in other genres and be well-rounded.

In the Bonuses section at the end of this book, I've included a link to a list of series in a range of genres, so you can find an example that's relevant to what you write and do your own reading. Of course, this is by no means exhaustive, but more of a springboard for your own research.

How to use this book

If you're anything like me, you might be tempted to skip ahead and read through the sections that are most relevant to you and where you're at in your career. However, I'd advise that you read cover-to-cover first and then revisit the sections that resonated with you the most. Although I've done my best to split topics into neat chapters and subsections, the truth is that a lot of this information is interlinked and will serve you best when digested in the overall context of the book.

So, shall we begin?

Section I: Understanding Book Series

"A word after a word after a word is power."
—Margaret Atwood, "Spelling"

ONE

The Basics of Writing a Series

"This is how you do it: you sit down at the keyboard and you put one word after another until it's done. It's that easy, and that hard."
—Neil Gaiman, "Pens, Rules, Finishing Things and Why Stephin Merritt Is Not Grouchy"

BEFORE WE DIVE into the nitty-gritty of actually writing and publishing in series, I want to cover the basics. I know, I know – chances are that if you've picked up this book, you probably know what a series is and you're keen to get to the good stuff. However, I want us to be on the same page (no pun intended) when it comes to the definitions, the different examples and the general impact a series can have on an author's career.

What is a series?

Put simply, a series is a set of connected novels or a multi-novel story that usually shares a common story arc, common characters and/or common settings. The books within a series are usually published in chronological order as to the events in the story.

A series can be a duology (two books) like *Six of Crows* by Leigh Bardugo, a trilogy (three books) like *His Dark Materials* by Philip Pullman, a quartet (four books) like *An Ember in the Ashes* by Sabaa Tahir, or even longer. The *Outlander* series by Diana Gabaldon (one of my favourites) spans nine books at the time of writing, with plans for a tenth and a prequel novel, while *The Wheel of Time* by Robert Jordan (and Brandon Sanderson) spans 14 volumes, as well as a prequel novel and two companion books.

Types of series

If you research different types of series, you'll find various definitions ranging from dynamic and static to standalone and episodic, as well as terminology based on the number of protagonists. (For a deep-dive into series types, I recommend reading Sara Rosett's book, *How to Write a Series: A Guide to Series Types and Structure plus Troubleshooting Types and Marketing Tactics*.) But for the purposes of this book, I want to keep things simple. For me, the "type" of series is very much dependent on genre, as you'll soon see. There are two main types...

Dynamic: This is the type most of us think of when considering series, where the story arc spans the course of multiple books. Each book builds upon the last, following the development of one or more characters and a timeline of events. For this reason, a reader needs to start at book one and cannot jump into the series at, say, book four. Usually, the characters undergo a transformation from who they were at the beginning of the series.

The dynamic series is most common in the fantasy and science fiction genres. Some popular examples are *Harry Potter, The Wheel of Time, The Witcher, Dune* and *The Maze Runner*, as well as my own works, *The Oremere Chronicles* and *Curse of the Cyren Queen*.

Static: In a static series, we follow the same character, but over the course of multiple books, that character remains much the same. They don't have a big metamorphosis as the series evolves. Instead, a static series is more like episodes or instalments, where each book contains a new obstacle or adventure that the protagonist must overcome before the end of the book.

The static series structure is most common in the thriller, crime and romance genres. Popular examples include the *Jack Reacher, Sherlock Holmes* and *Indiana Jones* series.

Outliers (or combinations): Of course, nothing is ever black and white, so there are certainly series that fit into both of the above types and borrow certain elements from one another. There are series that are technically static in that they follow a protagonist's story within a single book that's self-contained, while also using the same villain throughout the series (*Sherlock Holmes*), and series that focus on a single character per film, but bring them all together in joint ventures (*The Avengers*).

The key is to be able to spot the elements of each and to determine which type of series you're writing, *before* you start writing.

Series vs serials

One common point of confusion is the difference between *series* and *serials*. In the context of this book, we're defining series as stated earlier: a set of connected novels, whereas a *serial* publication is typically much shorter than a novel and isn't self-contained. While novels in a series have their own story arc, a serial story is more like a chapter of a full story arc that is part of multiple instalments.

A great example is *Great Expectations* by Charles Dickens. While we now know this as a full-length novel, it was originally published as a serial in the weekly periodical *All the Year Round*. Many Victorian novels saw success by being published as serials in newspapers. This form has evolved into modern-day web serials and with the introduction of Amazon's platform Kindle Vella. However, *this* book exclusively focuses on series of full-length novels.

TWO

Why Write in a Series?

"Creating a series can boost your author career and simplify your novel writing. You'll create benefits as a writer and increase your marketing power."
—Zara Altair, "Supercharge Your Author Career with a Series"

THERE IS a vast array of reasons to write in a series, ranging from the joys of craft to the financial benefits, and I want to explore them all with you. Remember, everything we discuss below should be viewed through the lens of long-term success. There is a long-term benefit to each point we explore – and success in this industry is all about the long game, my friends.

Writing in series is a strategy that's worked time and time again for the major success stories in our community, and one that has worked incredibly well for me personally. Once you start to understand *why* it works, you can utilise it more and more to your advantage, which is exactly what career authors do. These are authors whose careers span decades, whose novels make up the bulk (if not all) of their income.

So, let's not delay any further. *Why does writing in series work?*

1. The demand

If there was ever a time to understand the demand for and power of a series, it's now, in the age of binge-watching. As more and more books find their way to Netflix adaptations, series are more popular than ever before. Think of hits such as *Bridgerton*, *The Witcher*, *Virgin River*, *Shadow and Bone*, *Orange is the New Black*, *Gossip Girl*, *The Vampire Diaries*... the list goes on. These stories, along with many others, have tapped into hungry audiences, generating lively conversations and debates and loyal fandoms.

You only need to look at fan art, cosplays and fan fiction to understand how deeply people care for and rally around their favourite series. They create communities that allow viewers and readers to become part of something that's much bigger than themselves. Now more than ever there is a demand for escapist fiction, which is served best in series, whether it's books, TV shows or movies.

Our binge-watching tendencies, thanks to Netflix and its competitors, have definitely transferred to our reading habits as well. I know there is nothing I love more than settling in with a story that spans multiple books or episodes. People love the comfort of returning to the same settings and the same cast of characters, getting emotionally invested in what happens to them over the course of weeks, months and even years. It's like coming home to old friends.

A lot of the time, readers and viewers also grow up alongside a cast of characters, making them oh-so-easy to relate to. For me and a lot of my friends, a great example is Harry Potter. We were around the same age he was, and as the books were released over the following years, we and Harry grew slightly older with each one.

A good series also taps into one of the most basic human instincts: if something is good, we want *more* of it. It's also much easier to convince people to carry on with the characters they enjoy than to ask them to invest in brand-new ones. Personally, I often feel fatigued at the thought of learning about a new world and taking a new risk with unknown characters, whereas I'm more than happy to reach for my wallet if there's a sequel to a book I loved.

2. Utilise the groundwork

When you write a book, there is so much initial groundwork to be done. Whether you write fantasy, sci-fi, romance or any genre in between, there's intricate worldbuilding, a huge amount of setup, and painstaking work put into crafting and introducing your cast of characters.

Unless you're writing in series, you need to do this for every single book you write – starting from scratch, building your fictional world from the ground up. Writing in series allows you to utilise the initial groundwork you've done over and over again. You're not starting from zero every time you open a Word document or Scrivener file, and the further into your series you get, the more familiar you are with the world and its characters; you could walk through that world blindfolded and you'd find your way. That level of familiarity saves so much time when it comes to the writing process, and time is money, as they say.

Surely it makes sense to use that same world, those same characters again, right? Similarly to a reader finding comfort in returning to a familiar cast, an author can feel the same comfort when returning to write the following books in a series. I personally love working on later books in an existing series. This is when I already know the characters and it feels like we've been through a lot together. I don't have to constantly question what motivates them or why they would act in a certain way – I already know all this, which is incredibly liberating. It's times like these where you can sit down at the computer and the words just flow, and you write for the sheer joy of it. Crystal Hunt summarises it perfectly in her book *Strategic Series Author*: "This is the true power of writing a series. You're not starting over from scratch with every book. You're building on the successes of the previous book, and growing your skills and expertise around the world you've created."

3. The opportunity to explore

There's also something to be said for the magic that unfolds for the author while writing a series. Multiple books give us the scope to explore the nuances of our characters, the breadth of our settings and the epic scale of our plots with a lot more freedom than a single book ever could.

Despite having developed a strict outlining system in recent years, I've often found myself surprised at where a series has taken me, and I find immense joy in that; it fuels the creative process. As both an author and a reader, I love it when story arcs and threads woven throughout earlier books come together later in the narrative, and writing in series gives you that power.

The scope of a series also allows you the flexibility not to include every single thing in the first volume. You may have an array of ideas, but often newer authors make the mistake of cramming everything into their first book. A series forces an author to think about the breadth of the story and how it will span the course of multiple books, reassuring them that there is plenty of room later on to explore their ideas.

4. Money, money, money

One thing I've learned since publishing my first book is how lucrative series can be, which is something you need to nail down if you want long-term success.

Think about this: it's easier to convince a reader to read a sequel, or a book in the same series, than to get them to read something entirely new. When you write a series, you already have an inbuilt audience for the books that follow the starter novel. If you've written it well, people want to know what happens next and how things pan out for the characters. Put simply, you make more money per customer. If you only write one book, there's not a natural stepping stone waiting for the reader after they finish it. With each standalone book you publish, you essentially have to launch to a new audience over and over again. Of course, there are exceptions to this, like if you write in a genre where standalones are the expected form (for example, psychological thrillers or romantic comedies).

Once again, it's up to the author to understand the conventions of their genre and to do their own research. However, when we're talking about series, I always like to refer back to this gem from Craig Martelle: "Right up front, series are the cat's ass when it comes to profitability. When readers care about the characters who have given them an emotional high, the readers will stay on board, wanting more of their favorites. Give it to them. You've done the hard part of hooking them, now keep them on the line by feeding them more volumes." (*Pricing Strategies: Maximize your bottom line for long-term financial health*)

This becomes abundantly clear when advertising. In many instances you can create an ad for the first book in a series and reap the rewards of sales throughout your entire series, because readers have somewhere to go after they've finished that first book. Provided that your series has a solid read-through rate, it can be far more profitable in terms of advertising than a standalone title. And in fact, the longer the series, the better – but we'll get to that later.

5. Eliminate decision fatigue

The career of an indie author is rife with an array of daily decisions, so much so that we're often plagued with "decision fatigue". Sometimes, the smallest choices seem too hard to make, particularly if we're working solo day in, day out. This is one of the many reasons that writing in series can be so refreshing. For the most part, you always know what you're writing next, which means you're always looking and moving forward. This works for both the author and the reader; a series gives both parties a place to go next, providing a sense of direction and eliminating that often-overwhelming feeling of decision fatigue.

6. Promotional flexibility

Writing in series also gives you a lot more flexibility when it comes to promotion. In general, the more books you have in your catalogue the better, but series are particularly beneficial when it comes to rotating discounts.

For example, writing a series allows you to implement the "loss leader" marketing strategy, which means making the first book free or pricing it at $0.99 to hook readers into a much larger series, removing the barrier to entry. This has become a proven technique over the last decade or so of indie publishing, with six- to seven-figure authors like Elana Johnson, Lindsay Buroker and Mark Dawson all swearing by this method.

I've taken advantage of this strategy myself by using advice from David Gaughran's *Starting from Zero* course and running price promotions for the first (and sometimes second) book in a series, to cast the net as wide as possible and draw new readers into the sales funnel.

7. Taking advantage of "series pages" on retailers

Series pages are an often-underutilised tool. These are pages on a retailer website that are specifically for books listed in one particular series. Your series page acts as a great sales funnel, guiding readers from one book to the next, and often offers bundled discounts. As Craig Martelle says: "The series pages are cool. They help you sell more books because readers (those who like books in a series) can see the whole buffet table at one pop... you can add the series page (it gets its own ASIN) to your author dashboard so when you get a ranking, it shows up with the books in a series as opposed to single books." (*Become a Successful Indie Author: Work Toward Your Writing Dream*)

A series page also enables a bulk-buying feature for those who wish to buy the complete series with one click. You can create ads and social media posts that link specifically to this page, allowing you to target the series as a whole in your marketing and promotion.

————

To me, the power of the series form is undeniable, and the more I write and read, the more convinced I am that it's one of the best strategies for us indies. However, I appreciate that it's a daunting notion for many, and I want to address that in the next chapter.

THREE

The Resistance to Writing a Series

"Committing to a series, especially for a debut or new-ish author, is tough...
It's tough for a lot of reasons."
—Chuck Wendig, "Why Writing A Series (Especially As A New
Author) Is Really Goddamn Hard"

BEFORE WE MOVE ONTO TECHNIQUES, I want to address
one last point of contention: the resistance to writing in series.
Look, I get it: not everyone wants to write in this form, and
there's a handful of reasons for that. However, if that's you – if
you've been resisting this particular structure or are still on the
fence about writing in series – I want to address those concerns
now, because chances are, there's a way around them.

1. Your genre doesn't suit the structure

This is probably one of the most understandable concerns when
it comes to resisting the series structure. One of your main
responsibilities as an author is to meet your readers' expectations,
and that certainly extends to the structure of stories within your

chosen genre. I realise that not all authors love series and that not all genres work as well in series as, say, fantasy books do. A prime example of this is romance – romance readers like to have the complete romantic arc told within one book; they want to see the characters meet, fall in love, face some obstacles and, in the end, triumph over all else. So how can you satisfy readers in this regard, but also utilise the benefits of writing in series?

If you and your work fall into this category, don't worry – there are a few things you can do to position your books to share some of the benefits that series enjoy…

- Write interconnected standalones
- Write second-generation stories (more on these later)
- Write spin-off stories
- Write books set in the same location

These techniques allow your books to share a common thread without the same narrative spanning across multiple books, which provides a natural onward sale from one book to the next.

Two authors I've seen utilising one or more of these methods to incredible effect are J.R. Ward and Anne Malcolm. J.R. Ward's bestselling paranormal romance series, *The Black Dagger Brotherhood*, follows a guild of warrior vampires who live together and fight off their common enemy. However, each book is written from the perspective of a different warrior, and the main plot follows his love life. The series is chronological and the vampires' common enemy appears throughout all the books. Anne Malcolm's *Sons of Templar* series follows a similar pattern: it revolves around a biker gang, with each book in the series exploring a different member's love story. Both of these examples implement several of the above suggested strategies:

interconnected standalones, spin-offs, stories set in the same world and use of second-generation characters.

For a more mainstream example, just look at the Marvel Cinematic Universe. Each film stands alone, but they are all interconnected – there are constant references to the other films and cameos of various characters, and all take place in the same universe.

Successful indie Elana Johnson shares her experience in her book, *Writing and Launching a Bestseller*: "Develop your ideas into a series before writing the first book. I do this with a spreadsheet, and I utilize the family unit to do it. Most of my series are now family-based (new as of 2019), and they do far better than my pre-2019 series, which were loosely connected by a place (usually a ranch or a resort)."

2. It's a lot of upfront work

I'd be lying if I told you that writing series is easy. In fact, it's a huge investment of your time and energy from the get-go. This puts a lot of authors off, which is absolutely valid. However, as I touched on earlier, I personally believe that overall, writing in series *saves* you time and energy in the long run. While you might have to invest more time into building your world and story arc at the beginning of the process, you can utilise this work time and time again with each book in the series you write.

3. It feels like too great a risk

I can completely understand the feeling of risk associated with writing a series. I've experienced it myself on several occasions. Take *A Lair of Bones*, the first book in my *Curse of the Cyren Queen* series, for example... Before this title was released in July 2020, I had not only invested financially in its production (cover design, editing, proofing, etc.), but I had also written book two and outlined book three (a massive investment of time and energy). All that work and money, and yet there was a chance that *A Lair of Bones* might not earn it back, let alone make enough to turn a profit and warrant the production and publication of the following books in the series. There's no denying that I took a risk, and it certainly felt like one at the time. However, now… Well, now it's found its stride and its audience, and those readers continue to commit to new books in the series, wanting to know more about the main character's journey.

I wish there was something I could say to ensure your own risk pays off, but like a lot of things in this industry, sometimes you do just have to take the plunge. However, there are smaller things you can do to minimise the risk…

- Create a minimum viable product (the best book you can write with the time and resources you have) and track its success
- Don't invest heavily in advertising until more books in the series are out
- Get feedback on the manuscript as early as possible
- Work on building an audience with a relevant reader magnet (more on this later) *before* release to ensure the interest/demand for your story is there

4. There can be a higher barrier to entry for readers

As readers, many of us have experienced the overwhelm of a big series. I put off reading Diana Gabaldon's *Outlander* series for months because it was eight hefty books long (now it's nine). Sometimes, the length of a series can act as a barrier to entry for a simple reason: while a reader might have been initially attracted to, say, the cover of book eight, they realise they have to go back and read the initial books first. It delays the gratification and immediately increases the cost of entertainment (a very reasonable $4.99 might suddenly look more like $40). Series can also act as an emotional barrier – everyone is pressed for time outside of their regular life commitments, so readers may find themselves reluctant to commit to reading so many books.

However, I've found that over the course of a career, these things ebb and flow. A reader doesn't necessarily feel the same way from one day to the next, and the beauty of a series is that once you hook a reader, a lot of these barriers fall away. And trust me, there are countless "whale readers" out there just waiting to sink their teeth into a gripping series (more on these types of readers later).

5. Discouraged by experience of book one

Perhaps you've already tried the series route and were discouraged by the experience. Writing and publishing can be challenging in general, but series can have a unique way of kicking us while we're down. If sales aren't going well on book one, suddenly all the work we've done seems fruitless. However, in my experience, series can often take a little while to gain momentum. Readers want to see when the next book is coming out, or might even wait until the subsequent book/s are out to buy the first volume. They want proof you can deliver a story as promised, and don't want to be left hanging if they invest time and money in book one and there's no book two in sight.

If you've had a negative experience and you're considering leaving your series incomplete, I'd advise against it. Not finishing a series gives you a reputation of unreliability amongst readers, which is something you don't want. Instead, consider the following:

- Wrap the series up as best you can in the following book
- Ask current readers for feedback as to what's working and what's not
- Read your reviews to see if there's a common complaint (scary, I know!)
- Assess your branding (cover, description, categories) and determine if it's accurate and of a high enough standard

———

I can absolutely understand each and every one of these reasons for resisting writing a series. I've experienced most of them myself at one time or another. However, these fears and concerns are well worth combating if you're keen to build a solid foundation for a long-lasting career as an indie author.

Next, let's look at how to prepare for writing your series.

Section II: Series Preparation

"Read, read, read. Read everything— trash, classics, good and bad, and see how they do it. Just like a carpenter who works as an apprentice and studies the master. Read! You'll absorb it. Then write. If it's good, you'll find out. If it's not, throw it out of the window."
—William Faulkner in *The Paris Review* (Issue 12, Spring 1956)

FOUR

Write What You Love

"Don't write what you know, write what you're interested in, and you will never run out of ideas."
—Joanna Penn, *The Successful Author Mindset: A Handbook for Surviving the Writer's Journey*

I TRIED WRANGLING this section together many times before I realised I was struggling for a reason: the topics of genre, what we write, why we write and what we "should" write are very intricate and complex. There are a myriad of different reasons and countless more books on each subject. So for now, as we start to explore the preparation stage of writing a series, I want to delve into these ideas in the only way I know how: by telling you about my personal experience.

Writing is a constant, lifelong learning process, which means how and what you write will change over the course of your career, as it should. However, if you're serious about becoming a full-time author, or making a decent income from your books, you'll need to find the balance between writing what you love and writing what readers want. At its heart, that's all about genre.

Choosing the wrong genre

Let me take you back to 2013, a time when I was convinced that in order to be taken seriously as an author, I had to write literary fiction... Back then, I was freshly graduated from a degree in Creative Writing – which, while valuable in many ways, primed its students to veer away from commercial fiction and take the long-suffering, tortured artist approach to literature. I was young and impressionable, which meant I wrote a niche literary fiction book. It wasn't a bad novel. In fact, I submitted it to a number of publishers and it got a book deal with a small press. I signed a contract, drank cheap champagne and dreamed of one day becoming the next Cormac McCarthy or Anne Enright. But why?

My passion has always been the fantasy genre. Since I was a kid I've loved anything with magic and adventure; bonus points for stories that involved epic quests with strong female characters at their heart... So, why literary fiction indeed? Why was I forcing myself to write in a voice that wasn't my own, about characters I could barely relate to?

As I delved deeper into the production process with my new publisher, I slowly but surely began to realise that perhaps I'd ventured down the wrong path. I knew deep down that there was no way I could keep writing these kinds of books. I didn't have it in me to sustain a whole career on a genre that wasn't my passion.

In one of those fateful "blessing in disguise" strokes of luck, my publishing contract for said literary fiction book was cancelled. The small press wasn't doing well financially and after two years, before my book went to print, the rights were reverted to me. Despite the years of work and the prolonged frustration of the whole process, it was honestly the best thing that could have happened.

Why? Because somewhere amidst all the stress of working on a book I no longer loved, I rediscovered my passion for genre fiction – specifically fantasy.

Writing was suddenly easier. The way forward was suddenly clearer. Pieces of a puzzle that had remained a mystery to me for years suddenly fell into place.

Writing in the wrong genre for the wrong reasons is a trap many new authors fall into. I wrote literary fiction because of some warped desire for "prestige"; because as a female writer, I was aware of the ingrained misogyny of the literary world and wanted to ensure that I was taken seriously. I let these stigmas shape my work to a point where I couldn't recognise it. I also couldn't see past the current manuscript – there was no path laid before my feet after this particular book. Not ideal for someone who wanted a career as an author.

As soon as I turned to fantasy, that all changed.

Don't make the mistake I did of bowing to expectations, or paying attention to other people's "should"s, or being pressured by a hot trend.

I'll say it again: *write what you love reading.*

So, what is it that you love reading? Take a long hard look at the last 10 books (or more) that you really enjoyed. Which title kept you up past your bedtime? Which books were you still thinking about days later? Which book made you auto-buy the next in the series? What do these books have in common? Magic? Romance? An alpha male character? Cowboys? Warring brothers? Alien battles? Whatever it is that links them, identify it and explore it. This is what you should be writing.

Choosing the "right" genre

Choosing the "right" genre before you start writing is incredibly important for a number of reasons. Chiefly, genre is where *everything* starts. The genre in which you choose to write informs your entire premise, your entire narrative, the tropes you include and all your characters. It guides the direction of your whole series.

While we're not delving too deeply into marketing in this book, it would be remiss of me not to acknowledge that genre informs not only what you write, but how you market it. For example, the cover needs to be genre-appropriate; the blurb needs to highlight the "must-have" elements for that genre; the book needs to sit in the right categories and utilise the most relevant keywords... All of these details flag readers down, attracting them to your book – and if done incorrectly, you'll receive poor reviews and sales will tank.

If you get your genre wrong at the beginning, it's incredibly hard to go back and rectify it. Essentially, you'd need to start from scratch. It won't matter what you do with your marketing strategies or if you stumble upon a never-before-seen advertising method; if you've got the genre wrong, if you've misunderstood the tropes and reader expectations, you'll never be able to make that book work for long-term success.

Now, I've put the word *right* in air quotes in this subheading for a reason, and that's because there is no "right" genre. However, there *is* a right genre *for you*.

Writing what you love is crucial to starting down a path that will lead to long-term success, but that's not enough. I say *write what you love reading* with a caveat, because if it's your dream to become a career author, you need to do this *strategically*.

Picture two circles. One is what you love reading and writing; the other is a genre that sells. Writing what you love reading needs to *overlap* with writing what sells. There's a sweet spot in the middle.

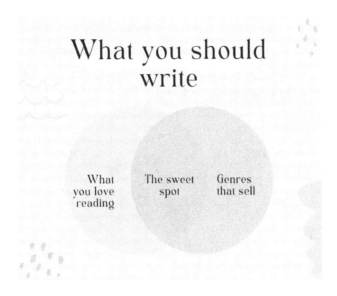

If you miss this sweet spot, you'll be as disheartened as I once was, potentially spending years of your life writing books no one wants to buy, or books you hate.

Remember, if you want to do this as a full-time career, you'll have to produce *numerous* books in a series and eventually an *entire body of work*, so there's no point in writing in a genre you don't like. If you do, that dream career you always imagined will start to feel like a nightmare. Believe me, I've been there. Those years that I spent on that literary fiction book were some of the most frustrating of my life. I could never have sustained a career as a writer of literary fiction.

If you want to make money, committing all your writing time to an obscure genre is also a huge risk, no matter how much you love it. No one will buy your books, and therefore there will be no royalties landing in your bank account. If you want to create something for art's sake, go right ahead – there are plenty of authors who write their passion projects on the side of their more commercial fiction. However, given that you've bought this book, you're here to learn about strategies for long-term author success, and that starts with choosing the right genre for you and your career. So let's get down to business...

FIVE

Do Your Research

"If you don't have time to read, you don't have the time (or the tools) to write. Simple as that."
—Stephen King, *On Writing*

REGARDLESS OF YOUR CHOSEN GENRE, I assure you that you'll need to do at least one form of research before you start writing your series. There's nothing worse than sitting down to put pen to paper only to be stumped by what you don't know. Research can be a matter of expanding a simple idea into a more thorough understanding of a topic, or it can be a launchpad for new ideas to flesh out a story arc that will sustain multiple books.

Research will vary for everyone. A writer of a historical fiction series might have months of research ahead of them, whereas a contemporary romance series might need very little. Before you start outlining or writing your series, you need to determine how much research needs to be done for your project.

In my experience, series research falls into one or more of the following categories: market research, worldbuilding, content research, craft research and inspiration.

Market research

"There are two methods of writing a book. You can write, then market. Or you can write to market. One has a much, much, higher chance of success than the other."

—Chris Fox, *Write to Market: Deliver a Book that Sells*

One of the most common regrets I hear from career authors is that they wish they had done more market research for their earlier works. This is certainly the case for me too. While I was a big YA fantasy reader at the time of writing my first series, I wasn't overly attentive to the overall market and the expectations that came with my chosen genre. It's a common mistake newer authors make: diving straight into writing without taking the extra time to familiarise themselves with the genre and market they're about to enter.

This isn't something to underestimate or to do by half measures. As Ricardo Fayet says in *How to Market a Book: Overperform in a Crowded Market*: "Marketing doesn't start when your book is finished. It starts before you even outline it. The first step toward creating a best-selling book is knowing exactly for whom the book is intended – in other words, knowing your market and writing to market."

If you haven't already started your own market research, or you feel what you have is lacking, now is your chance to get informed. Let's take a moment here to get familiar with the competition, the right tropes and the elements you need to turn your readers into fans for life. Where do we start getting to know the expectations and demands of your target market? With comp titles and series, of course!

Comparative titles and series

Comparative/comparable titles (or "comp" titles) refer to other books that are comparable to your own. For example, titles that sit alongside each other on the shelf of a bricks-and-mortar bookstore are often comp titles, as are books that are featured in the same particular genre or category of an online retailer. Comparative or "comp" *series* is just an extension of that for our purpose of studying the form, because I truly believe that if you're going to write in series, you should be reading series.

Let's look at a well-known example… *Divergent* by Veronica Roth is a comp title/series for *The Hunger Games* by Suzanne Collins. Why? Let's examine what they have in common:

- Post-apocalyptic/dystopian setting
- Districts/factions separating people/classes
- Same age bracket for target market (young adult)
- Strong female lead
- First-person narrative
- Trials/deadly games
- Political corruption
- Love story subplot

When you list the common elements like this, it's fairly easy to see why these two series are often compared to one another and why they're a fantastic example of a good comp title/series. Essentially, what it all boils down to is that these books share the same audience.

How to find your own comp titles and series

Don't worry – this can actually be quite an inspiring part of the research process. It's here that you can start to visualise where your book might sit on the shelves, and it may just act as a launchpad for new ideas for your series. However, if you're just starting out as an author, or the idea of market research is new to you, it can be a little overwhelming knowing where to start. So, here's where you can begin your comp title adventure…

- Look at the "Also Boughts" of your existing books on Amazon (the titles listed below the featured product as "Customers Also Bought") and the "Also Boughts" of *those* books
- If you're not yet published, look at the "Also Boughts" of the book you feel is most similar to yours, then look at *those* titles' "Also Boughts" and explore outward from there
- Visit the relevant categories on a range of retailers – for example, I often start with "Best Sellers in Teen & Young Adult Epic Fantasy eBooks" on Amazon. Then, study the bestselling titles and series in that genre/category. Read their blurbs and reviews. Which feature the most similarities to your own work?
- Go into an actual bookstore and browse the shelves of your chosen genre!
- If you're feeling super overwhelmed, ask your beta readers if they can think of similar titles
- Ask your author friends or post in an online community describing your work and requesting similar book recommendations

At this stage, I make it my mission to ensure that the comp titles I've been selecting are also part of a series. I start to pay attention to things like how many books are in that series and how well the following books are doing in terms of reviews and charts – nothing too granular, but just being mindful of those details on a general level.

If your genre isn't known for using the series form, see if you can find a successful author within it who *is* writing in series. Chances are, you'll find one. Look at their "Also Boughts" and reviews. Often, reviewers will mention other authors within their reviews; for example, "If you liked X, you'll love Y..."

Finally, a newer step I've added to my own market research is purchasing the relevant genre report from the lovely folks at K-lytics (I've provided the link to the website in the Resources section at the end of this book). Now, this is a paid service and not essential, so please don't stress if it's not in your budget. However, I found that it provided another layer of in-depth insight into my chosen genre and categories, and you can purchase the relevant report for a one-off cost rather than subscribing annually.

Now it's your turn...

Throughout this book, I won't be giving you a *tonne* of homework, but I'll make an exception here...

Choose five to 10 comparative series (remember: series that would sit alongside yours on the shelf) and *read them!* Ideally, these should be bestselling/high-ranking/highly reviewed series in your genre.

Yes, I do realise that this is no quick evening task. But if you've found that sweet spot between what you love and what sells, this homework *should be fun.* Keep sticky tabs or a notebook handy. If you're like me and you read on a Kindle, you can use the Highlight and Share functions to email yourself notes as you read.

What are we noting down while we read? Let's get stuck in…

Questions to ask about your comp series

- What do these have in common, both with each other and with your series idea? A strong female lead? A grumpy love interest? Royal courts? Monsters? Love triangles? Family rivalry? Make note of all of these.
- What is the common tense (past or present) and perspective (first or third person) used in your genre? Familiarise yourself with it. Can you write in this way? Are you a stronger writer in one or the other? Do you enjoy one more than the other?
- What is the common structure? Are the series dynamic or static? Do they follow the three-act structure?
- What types of endings do the authors utilise throughout the series? Cliffhangers? Happily-ever-afters?
- How many points of view are there? Single? Dual? Multiple? What is the reason behind this? What do you like and not like about the choices your fellow authors have made?
- Bonus: read the reviews of your comp titles! These are a goldmine of information and can spark inspiration. What tropes were used? What did readers love? What did they hate?

You'll start to see patterns in the answers above. Don't ignore these commonalities. Note any and everything down in the one place, be it a notepad or a research file on your computer. It doesn't matter if this is all over the place at the moment – we'll make sense of it later. However, your market research should be starting to inform your own ideas about your series and sparking new ones as you go. What you're creating here is an idea well of sorts: one that you'll come back to later to pick and choose from, and one that will inform the trajectory of your series.

Worldbuilding research

Whether you're writing an epic fantasy quest, a sci-fi adventure or a romance saga, knowing your world is crucial to planning for your series. You need to know if your series takes place in one setting, or if your characters will move around. You need to know the rules of the world and how big a role the setting plays over the course of multiple books.

This is where understanding your chosen genre comes in handy, because each genre has its own ways in which the story interacts with the setting and the broader world. For example, a common structure in fantasy series is that the first book takes place in the main character's homeland, where the reader becomes familiar with their version of normality. A conflict takes place in this homeland – a contained challenge or obstacle that the protagonist faces – before the end of the book sets us up to explore the rest of the world in the coming books.

For example, much of J.R.R. Tolkien's *The Fellowship of the Ring* takes place in our protagonist Frodo's homeland, the Shire. We get to know what hobbits are and how they live before Frodo is flung into a realm-wide quest.

In my own work, the entirety of *A Lair of Bones* takes place in the main character Roh's homeland: a lair of bones called

Saddoriel. Here, she participates in a deadly tournament. At the end of the book, her quest is extended and the story ends with a promise of exploring the realms further.

For otherworldly fiction in particular, maps are super useful when it comes to planning out where your series takes your characters (and your readers). At the planning stage for *A Lair of Bones*, I drew a very rudimentary map (which my designer would go on to perfect) and started charting the most logical course of travel for my main character and her companions. There was a lot of sketching in art pads and scribbling on whiteboards at the time. I still keep my fantasy maps pinned to the wall beside my desk for reference and consult them regularly when planning my series.

A lot of worldbuilding takes place during this part of the process, which is very intense in the fantasy genre. For me, the map played a crucial role as I find the physical movement within a story the simplest thing to plan first, before layering in the emotional and character-driven arcs.

Knowing your broader world, whether fantastical or contemporary, is crucial to the overall movement of your series. Planning how far your characters travel and where they are in which books will save you many headaches later, and will also help you set an even pace across multiple books.

You should also know the rules of your world, whether magical or otherwise. Will your characters be bound by the laws as we know them in our world, or are things different in your fictional setting?

Questions to ask about your world

- Is your world contemporary, historical, futuristic or fantastical?

- What period of time will your series cover and how will the world change throughout?
- What are the rules of your world? Magical or otherwise?
- How far does this world span? Do your characters travel across it? How so?
- Do you need a map?

If you're writing fantasy, I strongly suggest checking out Brandon Sanderson's Laws of Magic and the incredible list of worldbuilding questions from Science Fiction and Fantasy Writers of America, both of which you can find links to in the Resources section of this book. Both my questions and the more extensive resources provided can be used as templates or as a springboard for your own ideas.

Content research

Content research is information that will inform the events and plot points in your books. Some series, like those in the historical fiction genre, will require more content research than others. For example, author Diana Gabaldon had to research two vastly different historical time periods for her long-running series, *Outlander*. Her series is set in numerous locations across both the 18th and 20th centuries; this involved some of the most extensive research I've ever seen, including but not limited to historical events, wars and civil conflicts, locations, fashion, herbology, the evolution of medicine and hygiene... Honestly, the list is endless.

Perhaps you're not writing fiction based on historical events; perhaps you're creating a fantasy world entirely from scratch. General worldbuilding is also part of your content research, particularly if parts of this world or its rules inform your series arc. You may be using a medieval-inspired setting, which may require additional reading about architecture, weaponry and the hierarchy of royal courts.

Perhaps you're writing a medical romance series. In this case, you may need some basic knowledge about how a hospital and its various departments work before you can start planning and outlining your series arc.

All of these instances and those in between require some sort of basic knowledge before you can move onto shaping the overall arc of your series.

Questions to ask about your content

Depending on your genre and the nature of your research, you may have to explore both primary and secondary sources. Luckily, in this day and age, access to both types are at your fingertips. You can start with online searches, which may lead to books and experts to contact. The following are great questions to kickstart your content research:

- Is your series set in this world? Is it contemporary or historical? What do you need to know about this period of time?
- Do you need in-depth knowledge about particular real-life events such as wars or political movements?
- Do you need to know detailed information about particular types of weaponry?
- Do you need detailed information about a particular setting – be it large-scale like a country or small-scale like a hospital, industrial complex or small town?

- Do you need a basic understanding of current and/or futuristic technology?
- Do you need to know about the fashion of a particular era?
- If your series is set in a world other than the one we live in (e.g. fantastical, space, futuristic), what do you need to know?
- Do you need a map?
- Will your research inform the plot and characters? Is it relevant to the overall series? Is it something that can be layered in later?

Craft research

Depending on what stage in your author journey you're at, you may also feel underprepared in a particular area of writing craft, such as narrative structure, character development or creating conflict. Whatever aspect it may be, the research stage is the perfect opportunity to get extra reading done and build your confidence before starting down the series path. In fact, you're researching craft right now by reading this book!

Every author should always be striving to improve their writing, so this is something I do on a regular basis. There are new craft books coming out all the time and I like to keep a list of ones I want to read. During the research period, I return to this list and try to work my way through them. Often I find that these books give me new ideas for my story or prompt me to think in a different way about a certain character or plot point.

Questions to ask to refine your craft research

- Is there a craft element that reoccurred in your market research that you're unfamiliar with?
- Is there an aspect of your writing that critique partners have consistently given negative feedback on – for example, dialogue, pacing or structure?
- Is there a particular aspect of writing that you're insecure about?
- Is there a particular craft element you feel like you should know more about?

If you answered "yes" to any of these questions, it might be worth your while to find resources on that particular aspect and become more familiar with it. There is an abundance of books, YouTube videos and blog posts on just about every subject. I've included a brief list of my favourite craft resources at the end of the book.

Inspiration research

"Ideas are like rabbits. You get a couple and learn how to handle them, and pretty soon you have a dozen."
—John Steinbeck in *Cosmopolitan* (Issue 18, April 1947)

This is probably one of the most liberating aspects of the research process: the part where your inner artist comes out to play. This is what a lot of authors call "creative input". It involves anything and everything you do to spark new ideas and that flutter in your chest that feeds your excitement about your upcoming series. Researching for inspiration can be just about anything: gaming, exploring the great outdoors, creating music playlists, pinning images to boards on Pinterest to create a series aesthetic, watching films and TV shows, reading books in your genre.

Often we dismiss this form of research as we generally find it enjoyable, but let me tell you, it's just as valid as the others and can lead to some incredible breakthroughs in terms of ideas for your series. I've learned the value of this lesson many times over: "What I'm slowly realising is the importance of acknowledging the long game. Creativity that's not prioritised in these early stages of brainstorming and creation will come to be a major issue further down the line. Just because pen's not being put to paper and there are no words to be counted, doesn't make this aspect of the job less important or less of a priority." (Author Diaries, July 13th, 2019)

Questions to ask for inspiration

- What aspect of this project excites you the most?
- What do you want to learn the most?
- Are there any films/TV shows that could act as comp titles?
- Are there particular songs or playlists that inspire visions of your world?

Off the back of these questions, make a list of the various things you want to do to kickstart your inspiration. It might be that you want to binge-watch an entire season of *The Witcher*, or read the whole *Bridgertons* series. Maybe you want to visit a particular museum to better your understanding of a certain time period. You may want to create mood boards in Canva or a rough map of your fantasy world using Inkarnate (more on that later). Give yourself permission to work your way through the items on your list, taking notes along the way as inspiration strikes and revelling in the joy of your creativity.

The benefits of research

Doing your research in all of these areas *prior to writing* has several benefits that should be noted here...

1. You may discover that you're not particularly interested in a topic you had previously decided would be the backbone of your series. If this is the case, stop right there. If you're not interested in the research, you won't be interested in writing an entire series revolving around it. I've just saved you potential months and years of trying to make something work that would have sucked the life out of you (you can thank me later).
2. Similarly, your genre research might have revealed tropes and expectations that you as the author are uninterested in or are unwilling to meet. If that's the case, it's time to rethink the genre you want to write your series in.
3. Research may take you down several unexpected but intriguing paths that you may otherwise not have considered. These can fuel your creativity and create a much richer world for your series.
4. Having a foundation of knowledge will stop you stalling during the writing process where you might

be tempted to pause mid-draft and fall down a
Google rabbit hole.

What now?

For every single type of research you do, in every single session, you should be taking notes and saving resources in one place, collecting and compiling information to be used later. By now, the main thing you should know is what genre your series is and what type of series you're writing (dynamic or static). You should have a thorough understanding of your market and its expectations, as well as foundational knowledge about the world in which your series is set.

Now, we'll take this research and formulate a plan for your series…

SIX

Planning Your Series

"Planning is your best friend if productivity is your goal."
—Chris Fox, *5,000 Words Per Hour: Write Faster, Write Smarter*

SO, you've done a base layer of research and your mind is brimming with information, ideas and inspiration... Now we'll start to make sense of it all and begin to shape your research into a broader story arc.

Before we dive in, I want to pause for a brief moment to make sure we're on the same page when it comes to planning, because there's a lot of different terminology thrown around in the writing and indie publishing world. You're likely familiar with the *plotter vs pantser* dichotomy. If not, it simply refers to two camps of writers: those who plot/outline their books and those who "write by the seat of their pants", i.e. don't plan.

Regardless of what camp you consider yourself part of, I really believe that if you want to craft an addictive, seamless series that will contribute to the long-term success of your career, an element of planning is required.

Now, I don't mean to stifle anyone's creativity, so I want to be clear: this chapter specifically refers to planning in the *broader* sense of the series arc (read: this is not outlining – that's our next lesson, and I promise, there'll be info for pantsers too). This section is all about learning to expand upon your research in order to build a strong series arc that spans multiple books.

But first, how about a little confession from yours truly?

One thing I realised quite early in the initial stages of writing *Heart of Mist* and its sequels was that I hadn't done enough planning. I'm not referring to outlining in detail here (again, we'll get to that shortly), but rather a much broader part of the process – building the world and the characters to a point where I had a foundation strong enough to sustain multiple books without heavy rewrites and weeks of wasted time. That's what the diary quote in the previous chapter refers to: the initial brainstorming period where you throw all your ideas on the whiteboard and refine them from there.

While *The Oremere Chronicles* did well enough to kickstart my career, much of writing and editing those books was a painful, drawn-out process. When I started drafting *Heart of Mist* in 2016, I didn't plan the series. I knew vaguely where the story was headed and how I wanted the reader to feel when they reached the end, but that was it. I had no in-depth plans for how the books would unfold, how the story would progress across the span of multiple books, or even how my rules of magic related to anything. I had also made very little conscious effort to understand my series structure – I was just so eager to get those words down.

As a result, I was constantly running into issues where characters weren't where they needed to be for the upcoming conflict, or I'd written myself into a corner that needed some major reworking to get out of. It meant the stakes were so high at the beginning that it was difficult to continue raising them throughout the series, and that I had no understanding of how the magic used within the first book would be developed further later on. It also meant that the foreshadowing and various threads I wanted to weave together at the end weren't as well-executed as I would have liked.

You see, in order to include breadcrumbs and open loops (which we'll talk about in chapters 12 and 13), I needed to know what was going to happen in the books to come. This becomes a bigger problem if you're writing to publish immediately, by which I mean writing the book and publishing it before moving onto the next one. In that case, your words are set in stone and there's no reworking earlier books to get you out of trouble in the titles that follow. While I did manage to weave threads throughout all the *Oremere* books and draw them together in the final title, it was a challenge. The lack of overall series planning made the whole process stressful, to say the least, particularly as the books gained momentum and found their readership while I was scrambling to write them. Not knowing the trajectory of the series arc stalled my momentum and productivity, and I was writing far more slowly than I was capable of.

I don't want this to happen to you. So, how can we make sure your planning is solid?

1. Decide on your series type

We've discussed the types of series at length now, and you should know which category your series falls into: dynamic or static. This decision informs the structure of your entire series. For example, a dynamic series might follow the heroine across an entire realm in search of a magical object, while a static series might see a homicide detective solve a murder in each book. Without knowing your series type, you won't be able to move forward.

2. Brainstorm and refine your series arc

A series arc is the main overarching story that takes the reader from one book or episode to the next. It can be as simple as a single line. Here are some examples:

- *Harry Potter*: Will Harry defeat Lord Voldemort?
- *Bridgerton*: Will Daphne find a suitable husband?
- *Ozark*: Will Marty pay back the money and save his family?
- *The Dark Tower*: Will Roland make it to the Dark Tower?
- *The Lord of the Rings*: Will Frodo destroy the One Ring?
- *Mare of Easttown*: Will Mare uncover the killer?

Block out some time to brainstorm your own series arc. It could be an afternoon, a week or a month – whatever you feel you need to truly dig deep into the story. I'm talking about the big-picture plot points that tie multiple books together. Is it a big battle of good versus evil? Is it a place? A family? A master villain? A mystery?

Consider: what is the question the whole series is asking? Can good triumph over evil? Is Joe Average the best detective in the world? Can love conquer all?

Series arc vs book arc

A *series arc* is the bigger plot that informs the whole series. Each book within the series builds towards the resolution of this arc in the final instalment. A *book arc* is a storyline that is resolved in a single book. A series should have both a series arc and book arcs for the individual titles, but we'll get to that later.

So, how do you tell if your series arc is meaty enough to sustain multiple books? For some authors, this is a matter of instinct; they might experience a gut feeling or a hunch as to whether their arc is suitable for a series or not. However, for the rest of us, there are other ways we can find the answer.

The first place you should look is your genre (hopefully it's one where series are common) and its average book length. This gives you a rough idea of how many words a single volume in a series is expected to be. This is important in interrogating your series arc: can my series arc of "Hero tries to save world from tyrannical leader waging war" sustain seven 120,000-word books? Can my series arc "Jaded heroine who doesn't believe in love falls for billionaire boss" sustain three 60,000-word books? That's your starting point.

If you can't see how the arc could possibly fill out all those books, you need to ask yourself *why*. How can you develop the series arc to hold the weight of multiple books of a certain length? What other ideas do you have to flesh out the books?

Begin with the end. Knowing the destination of your arc will help you lay the foundations you need at the beginning and throughout. It should also make planning the individual books a little less daunting, as you'll know several plot points that need to happen in order to achieve the end goal.

3. Choose your subplots and tropes

Remember all that market research you did earlier? Remember how you wrote down the popular tropes and commonalities between your comp titles? Now you get to choose which ones you want to use and how you might adapt them to suit your own series. I'm not asking you to put them in order at this stage – just decide on what you might want to use. Subplots and tropes can be applicable to the series as a whole, a single book within the series, or even a single chapter or scene.

During the planning stage for *Curse of the Cyren Queen*, I knew I wanted to write an epic quest as the main story arc, but I also knew I wanted to include a tournament, the super-popular "enemies to lovers" trope and several magical artefacts, so I put all of these on my whiteboard.

4. Explore and develop your character arcs

Well-rounded characters are at the heart of any good series. They allow a reader to emotionally invest, to root for the underdog, to cheer on the couple and just about everything in between. If your main characters fall flat, no reader will continue past book one. Your characters need to be relatable and flawed; they need to have motivations of their own that drive the narrative forward.

For me, characterisation is often something I need to layer in during my structural edit, but I always want to have a rough idea of the overarching character arcs for the whole series before I put pen to paper. I ask myself the following questions...

Questions to ask about your characters

- Do your characters grow and learn throughout the course of your series? How?
- Are your characters flawed? Do they make mistakes?
- How do your characters react to the obstacles they face?
- Does your cast grow larger with the series? Why? Why not?

- Do you have enough characters to sustain the series? Do you have too many characters?
- Does the whole cast have their own motivations and goals?
- Is your protagonist active? Make sure they're not passive by default (where things just happen to them). Do they have their own drive and make their own decisions?

If you don't know the answers to all of these, that's fine. As I said, I often leave a lot of character detail until the later stages of editing. However, I always know where the character is heading, both physically and mentally. I know where they start and where they'll end up by the end of the series.

5. Finalise the core details of your world

At the planning stage, you should gather all your worldbuilding and setting knowledge in one place and create a solid foundation for your series. You need to decide on the key settings – where these are, what they look like, how they relate to other places and the rules of your world. If there's going to be travel in your series, you need a rough idea of how far this will span and how this is feasible for your characters.

I'm a big fan of physical movement across a series and exploring various places within the world, which is why I've always found it so useful to work with a map at this stage. It doesn't have to be professionally designed; just sketch it yourself to help you visualise characters getting from point A to point B.

6. How many books should your series be?

Unfortunately, this is one of those "How long is a piece of string?" questions, but it's certainly one you should be asking yourself during the planning stage of your series. To my understanding, longer series (upwards of five books) tend to be more lucrative when it comes to advertising and marketing, but it entirely depends on your genre as well. In some cases, the number of books in a series can be intuitive – for example, a romance that features five best friends might mean five books in the series, with each book focusing on one friend and their love interest. Detective series can be ongoing, with a new case per book. Fantasy authors tend to default to trilogies at first (which is exactly what I did) without understanding the benefits of longer series (which we'll explore later). Only you can decide what's right for you and your story, though we'll explore some strategies to keep your series length flexible later on.

When you're trying to plan your series, here are some questions you can ask yourself to help determine how many books you might need…

Questions to determine the length of your series

- Does my plan have strong enough story arcs and characters to sustain multiple books?
- Do I have enough passion for the genre and the story idea to sustain myself across multiple books?
- What are the bestselling authors in my genre doing? How many books on average are their most popular series?
- What is the passage of time throughout the series?

Does it span a year? Several years? A semester at university or school?

7. Take in the big picture

Planning a series is a huge task undertaken with a bird's eye view, which is why it helps to step back and assess the content you have at various stages. This is one of those stages. I like to ask myself the following questions:

- Have I got enough content to sustain multiple books? If not, what other obstacles can I throw in my characters' way?
- Is my series arc meaty enough to carry the reader from one book to the next?
- Can I combine ideas to make a better one?
- Is there an idea that now seems out of place amidst the others I've chosen?
- What is the main question of my series? (E.g. Will good triumph over evil? Will the main couple get together?) How do I answer this question?

More often than not, I find that I need more content at this stage – more tropes, subplots and character arcs. Perhaps I even bring in relationships and additional obstacles. I go through this process a few times until I step back and decide what I've got is a solid start.

8. Brainstorm with a trusted friend

At this point, I also recommend discussing your ideas with a trusted friend or partner – preferably someone who reads in your genre, or better still, a fellow writer. A fresh pair of eyes on your rough plan can help you spot inconsistencies, plot holes and parts that don't make sense or don't work in the context of the overall series. A fresh mind and in-depth discussion can help prompt bigger and better ideas. This step is one I've newly added to my own process, and I've found it to be an invaluable addition. Writing can be such a solitary job, and talking your ideas over with someone can spark new inspiration and motivation.

9. Don't let overwhelm win

Believe me, I understand the growing panic of overwhelm at this stage. But it's like that analogy of walking into a surgical theatre mid-operation: it's a mess until the doctor stitches the patient back together – only in this case, we're the doctor and our series is the patient. We'll make sense of it yet, don't worry.

Tools for planning your series

Call me old-fashioned, but when I'm planning and researching my series, my main tools are pen and paper and my whiteboards. On occasion I might use Post-it® Notes as well, so I can move things around if need be. I find staying off the computer for this initial stage (unless I need to Google something) incredibly helpful – it keeps me focused and I'm less likely to fall down a rabbit hole of internet searching when the priority is shaping the story. I make lists of things I need to look up later, but mostly, I just brainstorm. I write down everything I already know about the series, which usually prompts more ideas. I jot down any and all ideas until I hit the bottom of the well and need to generate new concepts. I take photos of all these notes and back them up in a Google Drive folder.

While I realise it's not an overly sophisticated system, it works for me, and I find the lack of computer time at this stage refreshing. Come writing time I'll be glued to the screen, so it's nice to have a little more freedom during the planning stage.

When I'm out of existing knowledge and my head is empty, that's when I start asking the questions like those we've explored in this chapter to help me expand my plan. You'll likely have noticed that asking questions is a common theme throughout this chapter. That is essentially what the planning stage of your series is about – asking questions and developing a foundation from which you can start to build your outline (or start writing if you're a pantser). Of course, some authors use more sophisticated tools than I do:

- Scrivener
- Notion, Asana and other task management apps
- Plottr
- Spreadsheets
- Templates (which we'll get to in Chapter Seven)

Once again, you need to experiment with what works for you and what suits your process best.

How long should planning your series take?

You probably already know what I'm going to say here: there is no right or wrong amount of time that this part of the process should take. Everyone is different. We all have different commitments, mentalities and goals. A series is more than a single idea. It needs time to percolate and grow, time to spark new ideas to sustain the creativity of the author and the interest of the reader. However, as you delve deeper into your career and write more books and more series, you'll likely see the need to streamline various stages of the writing process. You may come to find that you use research and planning as a form of procrastination, or the intensity of your efforts might induce fatigue on the topic before you've even started writing.

You need to find the balance between letting your ideas simmer and lingering too long in the pre-writing stage. Only you can learn this about yourself through trial and error.

Getting ready to outline (or write!)

If you take the advice in this chapter, you should have an incredibly strong foundation and understanding of the series you're trying to write. No, you don't have words on the page just yet, but you have a solid base of information to help when it comes to outlining and/or getting stuck into writing. None of what you've planned and researched is set in stone; these things change as you get to know your characters better, or as you learn more about your processes. But starting out prepared can only be a good thing. Doing this level of research, particularly when it comes to your genre, will help you down the line when it comes to marketing your work.

SEVEN

Outlining Your Series

"The more I know about the overall series, the more impactful I can make every big moment by leaving foreshadowing and such. It's still all a learning process – where to draw the line when it comes to planning the later books, but I've already done so much more than I ever did with Oremere.*"*
(Author Diaries, August 21st, 2020)

OVER THE COURSE of my career, I've learned that what works best for me is to outline. However, I completely understand that not all writers work this way. Different methods work for different people, so I've done my best to include information for plotters and pantsers alike. This chapter deals with the former and the one that follows is for those who prefer to write by the seat of their pants. However, no matter what camp you fall into, or if you have a tendency to be somewhere in between, I encourage you to read both chapters. To me, nonfiction books like this one are like a buffet: you can pick and choose what you want throughout, but you may also see something new you want to try.

This chapter is about outlining your overall series, not each individual book. It's completely up to you how detailed or broad you'd like to be. I'll be taking you through how I've come to outline my own series and how you can use or adapt the same method. I'll provide an outlining checklist and answer some frequently asked questions I get about this particular stage.

Again, if you're not an outliner, that's okay. But if you're interested in how an outliner might tackle the task, here we go…

Outline your series with me

After your initial planning and research period, you should have an array of ideas jotted down somewhere: ideas about plot points, character arcs, settings and more. The outlining stage is where we work out how all these elements fit into your series. Here, we're slowly going to make order out of chaos. We'll be taking things from your planning and research and roughly placing them where they should be in terms of the progression of your series. Of course, this might (and likely will) change as you shift gears into writing the books, but trust me when I say that knowing the general direction of the books in your series will be a lifesaver in the long run.

Be patient during this process. This is something I often need to be reminded of myself: "Outlining is a matter of building the story brick by brick – the foundation first, then the walls, the roof, etc. I keep getting frustrated with myself that the information isn't presenting itself to me in neat, chronological order, with all the finer aspects of character arcs and subplots laced throughout." (Author Diaries, August 14th, 2020)

For me, pieces don't always fall into place easily; I have to work at this task, give myself time and space to mull things over – that's when the magic happens.

So! Let's get started. On a big piece of art paper, a whiteboard or an app of your choice, I want you to create what I've decided to dub a "series blueprint". Don't worry – there's nothing complex about this (not yet, anyway). A series blueprint is a graphic or sketch (or in my case, a part of my office wall) that simply shows how each book falls under the umbrella of your series arc.

Write your series arc (that one line that asks the question of the overall series) across the top of your page. Beneath that, draw vertically placed rectangles to represent each of the books in the series – as many as you think you'll need: a trilogy, a quartet or more.

Depending on how crafty I'm feeling and how messy my desk is, I might do this using pieces of paper on my wall. For example, right now, I have nine sheets of A3 paper stuck to my office wall to signify each book in an upcoming series I'm planning. I particularly like this method because it allows me to physically step back and see the big picture.

The way you choose to do this isn't overly important, so long as you can see how your books fit into the series arc.

SERIES STORY ARC...

E.g. Will good triumph over evil?

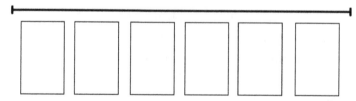

Once you've got something to work with, take a look at the planning and research you've done and start to move plot points and ideas into the books you think they need to occur in. This is why I like to do this exercise on my wall. I write points from my research and planning on Post-it Notes and physically stick them within the book rectangles. It also makes it far easier to move things around when needed. It's important to remember that nothing is set in stone at this stage; you're just playing with your ideas.

Personally, I look for patterns and start to place events in chronological order, and I try not to worry about the gaps at this stage. Again, it doesn't matter if this is messy, and it doesn't matter if it doesn't make sense yet. We're simply moving things around to see if they might work. I suggest you start with the big plot points and work out where they might roughly sit within your overall series arc.

Next, hopefully you'll have brainstormed some subplots and character arcs to use throughout your series as well. Now it's time to think about where they might work best. These might span across some of the books in the series, but not all. Depending on how you're sketching this out, place the subplots and character arcs in the relevant books. I find colour coding particularly useful for this stage. For example, on my current series blueprint, I have pink Post-it Notes for any romantic subplots (yes, I know it's clichéd, but also easily recognisable). So for books one to three, there is a pink Post-it that says *Romance #1 – Forbidden Love*. That's it, at least at this early stage. I also have an orange Post-it to signify the common main setting of those first three books and a blue Post-it for the gradual unfolding of a dark truth...

SERIES STORY ARC...

E.g. Will good triumph over evil?

I find visuals particularly helpful when I'm trying to outline the broader plot points of my series, but some people might prefer spreadsheets, notepads or a software like Plottr. It might take a while to find the format that works best for you, so be patient with yourself and lean into the trial-and-error element. You'll find the right match eventually.

Whatever medium you choose to use, repeat this exercise of placing information within the various books, including all your subplots and character arcs, until everything you've discovered through your planning is plotted on your series blueprint.

For the most part, I find a place for each of the subplots I have, and roughly know where I'll be placing certain tropes – whether these span several books or a single scene. I keep doing this until I've worked my way through all my planning material.

SERIES STORY ARC...

Will Roh succeed and win the cyren throne?

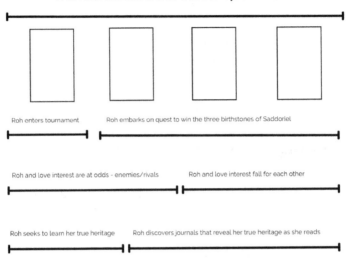

Roh enters tournament   Roh embarks on quest to win the three birthstones of Saddoriel

Roh and love interest are at odds - enemies/rivals   Roh and love interest fall for each other

Roh seeks to learn her true heritage   Roh discovers journals that reveal her true heritage as she reads

Of course, as you do this exercise, you may find that some things you had planned for are no longer relevant, or now don't work in the context of the overall series. Keep these details saved in a folder or a notebook to return to – you may find a use for them later as more of the story and the characters are revealed to you when you start writing. I often find I can repurpose ideas later down the line, or even save them for a future series.

Next, we're going to examine the inciting incident, midpoint and climax of each title in your series. But first, for those who might need a quick refresher...

- **Inciting incident:** The event that sets the narrative and the main characters in motion
- **The midpoint:** The major plot point that occurs roughly in the middle of the story. This usually brings

the protagonist closer to or further away from their goals
- **The climax:** The dramatic turning point of a narrative where the main conflict is resolved

Here's how these look for the first four *Harry Potter* books...

Harry Potter and the Philosopher's Stone

- **Inciting incident:** Hagrid introduces Harry to the wizarding world
- **Midpoint:** Harry's broom goes haywire during Quidditch and it becomes clear something deadly is afoot
- **Climax:** Harry, Ron and Hermione attempt to obtain the Philosopher's Stone

Harry Potter and the Chamber of Secrets

- **Inciting incident:** Harry and Ron miss the Hogwarts Express and fly a magic car to school
- **Midpoint:** Harry finds Tom Riddle's diary and learns more about the first time the Chamber of Secrets was opened
- **Climax:** Harry discovers that Tom Riddle is Voldemort

Harry Potter and the Prisoner of Azkaban

- **Inciting incident:** Harry is attacked by a Dementor, one of the guards of the prison from which Sirius Black escaped
- **Midpoint:** Harry discovers that Sirius Black is his godfather and betrayed his parents to Voldemort
- **Climax:** Harry and Hermione use a Time Turner to go back in time and save Sirius

Harry Potter and the Goblet of Fire

- **Inciting incident:** Harry's name is drawn as a fourth champion in the Triwizard Tournament
- **Midpoint:** Harry manages to complete the first Triwizard task and everyone realises how dangerous the tournament is
- **Climax:** Harry witnesses Lord Voldemort's return and discovers Professor Moody is a Death Eater in disguise

I suggest you come up with the inciting incident, midpoint and climax for each of the books in your series. It's absolutely fine to have these in simple dot points, but this is the stage where you need to iron out these details as best you can. Again, these are not set in stone, but it helps to give yourself a sense of direction for each book so you can see the movement of events across the series.

Once you have done this exercise, examine how each book

relates to the series-long arc, i.e. how each book contributes to the overall progress made towards the end goal. For each book, ask yourself:

- How does the main character grow and/or change?
- What question does the book answer?
- What question does it ask in order to lead into the next volume?

Here's how this looked for my series, *Curse of the Cyren Queen*:

- *A Lair of Bones*: Roh enters and wins the tournament, but there's an additional quest! Will she accept the challenge?
- *With Dagger and Song*: Roh seeks and finds the first gem, but will she get the next one?
- *The Fabric of Chaos*: Roh seeks and finds the second gem, but will she get the last one?
- *To Wield a Crown*: Roh seeks and finds the last gem, but will it be enough? Yes, but not in the way the reader thinks

All four books ask and answer their own question, but also come together to progress towards the ultimate goal, which is Roh winning the cyren crown.

A series, particularly a longer series, houses multiple story arcs and subplots to help sustain the reader's interest across multiple books, so that's where I started. I knew that each book should answer a major question, but ask another before the end.

For *Curse of the Cyren Queen*, I liked the idea of trying a quartet rather than a trilogy (in my mind I was going to build up to writing longer series gradually). So I sat down and brainstormed how I could spread this story out over the course of four books. I decided that book one, *A Lair of Bones*, would be contained to the protagonist's homeland, so the reader could get to know her sense of normality before the main part of the quest began. I brainstormed various tropes and story arcs and decided that *A Lair of Bones* would revolve around the tournament trope, where the protagonist, Roh, faces three deadly trials as a means to throw her hat in the ring as future queen. After Roh faces these challenges, a particular clause in the tournament rules is put into play that means the fight for the throne has only just begun. To prove herself worthy of the cyren crown, Roh must collect three magical gems that have been scattered across the realms. Thus, each following book is centred around the retrieval of one of these gems and takes our protagonist into the wider world, following a set formula for each instalment.

These decisions immediately helped to shape the broader structure of my series; they gave me a main plot point for each book and a formula to follow. It was as though I were looking at my series from a bird's eye view and could see the way forward easily.

For me, this part of the process often feels like filling in the blanks and fleshing out the meat of the story over the skeleton. Once I knew those simple arcs, it was a matter of bulking out the details and getting to know the characters and their motivations, which inform numerous subplots that span multiple books. I questioned how these could fit into my series – which ones would be carried across the whole arc and which would be resolved, used to reward the reader within each book for sticking with Roh and her unlikely crew. If I found the tank empty, I returned to brainstorming and researching in the hope of sparking new ideas.

One thing I often chant to myself as I'm planning is this quote: "In the first act get your principal character up a tree; in the second act, throw stones at him; in the third, get him down gracefully" (*Bridgeport Herald*, 1897). Only my version is a little more aggressive: get your main character up a tree, throw rocks at them, and then... *set the tree on fire.*

No matter what genre you write in, there should always be challenges and obstacles for your characters to overcome, and outlining is all about finding these elements and placing them in the series arc where they sing best.

Questions to ask yourself about the progression of your series arc:

- Does each book raise the stakes from the last instalment?
- Does each book contain its own complete arc within the series?
- What is the question of each book in the series? How do you answer this?

Once I've got my series outline as mess-free as possible, I like to review it with my partner. He has a way of asking questions I would never think of that prompts new ideas and generates new energy for my series. If you have the opportunity, I strongly encourage you to talk your outline over with a trusted friend or partner for these reasons. Sometimes it's good to leave the writer cave and get some outside input and a fresh pair of eyes on our plans.

Outlining checklist

- Compile all your notes from planning and research
- Create a separate list for each book and put in the relevant information you already have
- Brainstorm and decide on the inciting incident, midpoint and climax for each book in your series
- Fill in the blanks where you can with leftover planning material
- Return to research to seek new inspiration if you're unsatisfied
- Add to the series outline until you're happy with the level of detail

- Review your series outline with a trusted brainstorming partner

How much of the series should you outline?

Personally, I've come to learn that outlining in more detail works best for me. For example, for each book in my series, I generally try to have at least a sentence written down for each chapter, along with the main plot and character arcs; this helps me layer in foreshadowing, open loops and breadcrumbs (which we'll discuss at length shortly) and leads to a well-executed (and hopefully addictive) series. However, I understand this method isn't for everyone, and we'll get to some alternative options shortly. How much you outline is entirely up to you and how you work best.

If you *are* an outliner and you're planning on a shorter series like a duology or a trilogy, I'd suggest outlining the series in more detail, including subplots and tropes. In a shorter series you don't have the luxury of more than three books to weave everything in; it's contained to a smaller arc, and so it's best to know as much as you can upfront.

If you're planning to write a longer series, you need to make a strategic choice here about how you structure your series and how much of it you outline. We'll talk about this in more detail later, but as a precaution, I'd suggest outlining in sets of threes or twos – so, if you were writing a nine-book series, you may have three linked trilogies that each have their own narrative arc. In this case, you'd outline the first three books in more detail and then jot down rough dot points (at the very least: inciting incident, midpoint and climax) for the subsequent six titles. This is so you don't put hours and hours of work into outlining a series that may change or that you might find better suited to a shorter length once you start writing. Outlining and writing in linked trilogies and duologies also offers you an escape route if needed – it creates a way out if a series doesn't do well and you don't want to continue writing it further down the line.

If you want to outline in more detail but feel stuck or overwhelmed, I recommend using a template (more on this shortly) to flesh out the content of each book. This ensures that you have enough to work with as the series progresses. Remember to review the series arc in chronological order and ask yourself: are there plot holes? Timeline issues? Do the characters change and progress? Is there an obviously weaker book? Then, address these and book in a session with your brainstorming partner, where you can run through the whole series arc along with any overarching subplots and character arcs. Once you're happy with the general trajectory of the series, you can focus on the outline of book one (if you wish to outline).

How detailed should your outline for each book be?

Unfortunately, this is yet another "piece of string" question. My outlining process is one that has developed over several years and is constantly evolving as I write more series. I've learned something new every time I've published and I try to implement these lessons with each new project. You need to use trial and error to discover what works for you personally and refine the process as you go. Elana Johnson hits the nail on the head in her book *Writing and Marketing Systems*: "You don't know what you can do until you know what you can do, and the only way to find out what you can do is to try it, test it, track it."

How much detail you go into – whether it's more of a general plan, or if you prefer to outline down to the last grain of sand – is up to you. Only you can know what will fuel your creativity and productivity and what will stifle it. As the author,

69

it's your responsibility to figure out how you work best and apply your own methods.

What if you want to outline but you're stuck?

If you're anything like me, sometimes you might feel like a deer in headlights when you're expected to come up with all the events for a series or a book at once. If the idea of outlining an entire series is causing you serious overwhelm, I've got another piece of advice for you...

Find a formula that suits you and your genre.

If there's one thing that has irrevocably changed my outlining and writing process for the better, it's finding an outline template to follow. One of the best things I ever did was use Derek Murphy's "One-Page Novel Plot Outline" for the books in the *Curse of the Cyren Queen* series. I used it as a blueprint to guide my own ideas into a coherent narrative arc for each book and found the process kept the overwhelm at bay.

This outline splits each book into 24 chapters, and I generally try to do this on a dot point level (so each book has roughly 24 points) before I create a far more detailed (almost scene-by-scene) outline for the first book. In doing this for the later books too, I discover which story arcs I need to begin weaving in early to create that dramatic payoff later. This outline changes as I develop the series and start writing – for example, none of my books are actually 24 chapters long – but I find it's a strong starting point for me.

When you're stuck or overwhelmed, adhering to a formula can take away some of that paralysing decision fatigue and give your books and series instant structure. Some templates you could use are:

- Derek Murphy's "One-Page Novel Plot Outline" (based on the three-act structure)
- Jessica Brody's *Save the Cat! Writes a Novel* (has templates for a variety of genres)
- Gwen Hayes' *Romancing the Beat: Story Structure for Romance Novels*

You can also do your own research to find outline templates that suit your own brief and particular genre. I should emphasise that you don't ever need to follow a blueprint point by point. You shouldn't feel like it's cheating or stifling your creativity; when used correctly, a formula or template should stimulate and generate your own creative ideas. Use it as a rough skeleton and shape it to suit your own process, not the other way around.

Find a formula that *works for you* and use it consistently throughout your series. You'll find that it might increase your efficiency; you won't have to teach yourself how to write a book each time, and it'll save you time and energy (and likely many headaches in your structural edits). If plotting suits your personality and methods, refining this process over time will help you streamline your production, which can only be a good thing for a career author.

However, if you've read through this rather lengthy chapter thinking, *This isn't me*, then the next chapter is for you – we'll talk about how to approach writing your series as a pantser. But plotters, stick around: you'll find some gems relevant to you as well. Let's get cracking…

EIGHT

Approaching a Series as a Discovery Writer

"When I'm writing a novel, what comes first is an image, scene, or voice... The structure or design gets worked out in the course of the writing. I couldn't write the other way round, with structure first. It would be too much like paint-by-numbers."
—Margaret Atwood in *The Paris Review* (Issue 117, Winter 1990)

THERE ARE many successful novelists who *don't* outline their series before they start; these authors are called "discovery writers" or "pantsers" (those who "fly by the seat of their pants"). Diana Gabaldon, George R.R. Martin and Margaret Atwood all fall into this category, along with many more. In the introduction to his *Dark Tower* series opener, *The Gunslinger*, Stephen King tells us how fans wrote to him from death row and their sickbeds, asking to know how the series ended before they died... King explains that he would have granted these dying wishes if he could have, but: "I had no idea of how things were going to turn out with the gunslinger and his friends... To know, I have to write." This aptly summarises the approach of many discovery authors. They allow the story to unfold naturally as they write, unrestricted by an outline.

For this chapter, I spoke to some successful indie discovery writers, including epic fantasy author, David Estes, and USA Today bestselling author, Krystal Shannan, to get their perspectives on writing a series with this approach.

How pantsers approach writing a series

Discovery authors approach writing a series very differently to those who outline. Many begin with a concept, like Margaret Atwood in the opening quote of this chapter; she starts small, with an image or a scene, and works outwards from there.

Others start with a degree of planning. David Estes, author of *The Fatemarked Epic*, was kind enough to share his process with me: "Being a pantser, or discovery writer, while attempting to write long, epic series with large casts of characters can, at times, feel like climbing a mountain without a rope. Which is why my process requires a fair bit of upfront work, even if it falls short of preparing any sort of formal outline. For my latest two epic series, *Fatemarked* and *Kingfall*, I've followed a very similar process."

David goes on to explain that he uses four poster boards on his office wall that include the map, key characters and royal lineage, the magic system and his world's history. "Typically this is a summary of at least 500 years of world history, including significant events (wars, treaties, expansions, alliances, inventions, etc.) and provides a clear timeline for how the world became that way that it is at the start of my story."

Then, without an outline, he starts writing. He uses random "stream of consciousness" notes that he has compiled in the weeks and months (sometimes even years) prior to starting the draft, and slowly begins to organise these in the correct order as he writes. He tells me, "Some ideas never make it onto the page, and are either deleted (because I realize they suck), or are set aside to potentially be used in another book (because they don't suck)."

So, David and I are actually quite similar in that way, despite the fact that I'm an outliner and he's a discovery writer.

David Morrell, thriller author and the creator of the iconic character Rambo, has a similar approach: "I like to think of the book as being an adventure... The way I do it is I know the beginning and I'm really excited by it, and I know the big scenes, and I know the ending, and then I go in each day and I say, 'All right, surprise me. Story, tell me what you want.'" ("David Morrell & Ken Follett Talk About Writing", 2010)

In an interview on *The Creative Penn* podcast, author Patricia McLinn describes a similar starting point: "I don't plot ahead of time. I dive into the book, writing whatever I know at the time. And for me, most of the times the books start with almost like I'm eavesdropping on two people in a restaurant."

Krystal Shannan, who has written numerous series in the paranormal romance genre, tells me that she holds most of her information and plans for her series in her head, at least at first. Then it's a matter of creating sparing notes and eventually writing down more detailed information in the novel writing software, Scrivener. She says: "I usually build out a glossary when necessary as well. I also use a timeline software call[ed] Aeon2 to track the events in the book. And I track book structure with a sticky-note wall outline that shows me where I am and what has happened and what turning point etc. I'm at in the book. So every time I finish a chapter, I add it to the wall and adjust trajectory of next chapter if necessary."

I found Krystal's strategy of mapping her chapters in real

time as she writes fascinating, and I can absolutely see how this might help her keep track of everything without the daunting upfront work of creating an outline.

Another aspect of Krystal's process that interested me greatly was her approach to the overarching conflict of her series:

> Typically for a series, I personally build around a 'big bad' of some sort. So I know what their end goal is even if I don't know how they plan to do it at the very start. And even when I say I don't know, it's more of a[n] 'I don't know yet'. It's up there in the ocean of my brain being put together by my subconscious. And when it fits, when I find the right piece for the puzzle, the light goes off and I write until it's too dark to see where the story goes next. Then the process starts all over again. Me poking around in the story with a flashlight looking for the path.

The development of a "big bad", as Krystal calls it, is a key point here. While she doesn't outline, she still builds an antagonistic force that affects the trajectory of her series.

The benefits of pantsing a series

One of the common benefits of pantsing I'm frequently told of is the thrill of discovery. Many authors who use this method revel in using their intuition and the liberation of the act of writing itself. David Estes tells me one of the biggest joys he experiences as a pantser is: "Being surprised when the ending of a book or the series as a whole turns out to be completely different (and so much better) than I originally imagined it. The excitement of the 'Aha!' moments... that suddenly connect the threads I've been struggling to connect for days or even weeks. These moments feel like your favorite team winning the Super

Bowl, winning the lottery, and opening Christmas presents all rolled up into one."

Experiencing these connections and "aha" moments is a common pleasure for discovery authors. Krystal Shannan also lists the excitement of discovery as one of the aspects she loves most about this approach to writing:

> I love feeling the characters' joys and sorrows as they move through their stories. Most of the time, I have no idea exactly how a scene is going to go until I sit down to work on it. I might know that we have to get from Point A to Point B [be]cause that would be a nice place to land, but that's usually about it. I might know that they need to talk to someone, but I'm not sure about what. I usually know that I'm working toward a high point or a low point. It's exciting and one of the best adventures.

Writing with abandon can also help newer writers discover their voice and style and develop deeper emotional themes in their work. Pantsers are also able to enjoy the flexibility to make changes as they write.

Combating the challenges of writing a series as a pantser

As with all writing, there are inevitable challenges to approaching a series as a pantser. As an outliner, one thing I personally struggled to understand about discovery writers was how they write if they don't know where the story is going. In our chat via email, David Estes told me that this does indeed sometimes cause an element of stress, which "can quickly turn into full-blown writer's block if you're not careful". However, he went on to explain that he combats this "by focusing less on the big picture and more on the individual plights of each character, burrowing deep into their needs, desires, motivations and emotions to fully immerse myself in their world". This approach keeps him inspired and the creativity flowing.

Another technique David uses to prevent feeling blocked is to finish each writing period "by adding a series of notes to read before the next writing session", which helps prevent the often daunting feeling of the blank page the next day. It also enables him to "jump right back into the story the next day with minimal need to read what I wrote the previous day. More writing time means greater productivity". It's not the first time I've heard this method described by an author.

Other pantsers have suggested creating an emergency road map for the plot in the event that they find themselves completely blocked. Krystal Shannan tells me that having the knowledge that she can return to the manuscript at any time and fix mistakes helps her overcome the fear of making them: "I think just knowing that ahead of time and being willing to fix it is a huge thing. Knowing that my best process works this way. My best, most exciting and thrilling books are written this way – discovered by me and the characters in the same moment."

Throughout my research and in discussions with various discovery authors, other problems mentioned were including foreshadowing and breadcrumbs, as well as avoiding plot holes and continuity issues. These are all challenges I face even as an outliner, so I was curious to know how a pantser might address these concerns. David tells me he usually has a few "big twists" at the ready in his notes to be used throughout the series, but that he also holds off on publishing the first book as soon as it's finished for this reason: "I generally write at least the next two books (say, in a five-book series), which allows me to go back and make changes/additions to book one. So if I have one of those

'Aha!' moments I spoke of early when I'm in the middle of writing book three, it's not too late to sprinkle some hints throughout the first two books before the big reveal in book three."

He also credits his beta reader team (comprising of six to eight readers) who help "ensure the overall cohesiveness of the series and that any plot holes have been filled in before I publish". This is a technique I use as well. Ideally I have the same two to three beta readers, who are intimately familiar with the series as a whole and can help me spot inconsistencies and plot holes.

Krystal Shannan explains that her approach to foreshadowing is to use "tons of threads and open loops and breadcrumbs", many of which she doesn't quite understand the meaning of at the time. It's not until later that things click into place for her. She tells me, "I'll get to a point later in a story and go 'Oh! That's why they did that earlier!'. So, I have all those things in my first drafts. I personally, rarely have to go back and add those in later."

———

Of course, there's no way we can divide all authors into two simple camps. There are those who don't identify with either method and those who fall somewhere in between. The key is to find the method that works best for you – that not only sparks your creativity, but enables you to get the book written, and the next, and the next.

As someone who has both written a series *without* outlining and written a series *with* outlining, for me it came down to how much work I wanted to do upfront versus how much work I had to do at the end.

With *The Oremere Chronicles*, the process was drawn-out and painful due to my lack of forethought. With *Curse of the Cyren Queen*, the process became quicker with each book as I learned to identify my common mistakes and weaknesses within each outline. I was able to address these issues before writing over 100,000 words, which resulted in a far more streamlined process for me. As I honed my outlining techniques, each book became stronger than the last in terms of overall pacing, structure and character arcs.

However, you might experience the opposite. An outline might drain your creativity; plotting may cause you to lose interest in the story. Perhaps you'll find that you prefer a happy medium of the two methods. The key takeaway here is to learn what works for you and to keep learning, keep optimising, so that each book and series will be better than the last.

So, when do we get to the actual *writing* part of writing a series? Right about now.

Section III: Writing Your Series and Must-Have Elements

"The first draft is just you telling yourself the story."
—Terry Pratchett, quoted in Sue Hertz, *Write Choices: Elements of Nonfiction Storytelling*

NINE

It All Starts with Book One

"The scariest moment is always just before you start."
—Stephen King, *On Writing*

FORGIVE me for stating the obvious, but everything about your series hinges on the success of the first book. Let me explain...

The sales figures of your series starter determine the sales of the rest of the series. Only a certain percentage of people who read book one will go on to read book two; only a certain percentage of those readers will go on to read book three; and so forth. This is the nature of all series publishing.

It's a scary concept, especially considering that it's quite natural for the quality of our books to improve the further into the series we get. As we progress through the series, our understanding of the world and the characters grows, and we learn more about our own processes and weaknesses – not to mention we should always be striving to improve. Although I'll always have a soft spot for my debut, it's certainly not the best of my books – that's always the one I've written most recently. It can be a mental hurdle to overcome, knowing that you'll be judged on that first book, despite the fact that the following books will likely be stronger. However, there's a solution to that, which I'll discuss in the section on "literary universes".

The significance of that first book in *The Oremere Chronicles* wasn't something I thought about pre-publication, or even while I published its sequels, *Reign of Mist* and *War of Mist*. However, in more recent years, it's a lesson that has ingrained itself in my mind, but one that I don't think is often talked about in detail when discussing writing series…

> I've been watching V.E. Schwab's interview series "No Write Way" and in the episode with Jay Kristoff, they're talking about the trajectory and gravity of a series, how the first book always sells the best and then it's a natural downward slide from there. Which I knew from tracking TOC sales, but they said it so articulately that it refreshed my desire/need to make Lair of Bones the absolute best it can be. It's worth spending more time on it when I get it back from betas to ensure that, even if I have to push back the cover and edits. There is always this ticking clock within me that says I need to work faster, release books faster, but the truth is, I've bought myself time to get this book, this series, right. (Author Diaries, April 29th, 2020)

In the journal entry above, you get to see the penny drop in real time: this was the moment when I first understood just how vital the first volume in a series is. In my research for this book I discovered that the original video on V.E. Schwab's Instagram account has been taken down, but you can now find the episode in podcast form: "Dark by Nature, Interview with Jay Kristoff" on *No Write Way with Victoria V.E. Schwab*.

When I published my first series starter, although I had done Mark Dawson's Self Publishing 101 course (highly recommended for beginners), I didn't have any author friends in the indie space. I had no one to compare numbers with, no one who understood the lay of the land and essentially, no real way (besides looking at my royalty reports) of knowing how things were panning out and what was the norm. What I've learned in hindsight is just how well that first book did. It has only been in recent years that I've come to understand how the success of *Heart of Mist* set the bar for how the rest of the series performed.

I'm giving you this background story not to pile the pressure on, but to impress upon you the importance of crafting a series with intention from the start. Your series opener will set the stage for the rest of your series, not only in terms of your story arc and character development, but for your sales and financial success.

So how do you ensure a strong start for your series?

1. Provide a complete story arc

Although a series is an ongoing story arc, it's important that each book contains its own complete narrative that leaves the reader satisfied. You need to be able to prove to your readers that you can write a complete story. As K.M. Weiland points out in *Structuring Your Novel: Essential Keys for Writing an Outstanding Story*: "Each book within a series must adhere to its own individual structure just as clearly as if it were a standalone book... Climaxes must still present a definitive outcome and usually at least a partial victory."

If a reader is left dissatisfied with an incomplete story arc in book one, they're not going to read the second and third instalments. As always, depending on your genre, there will be certain expectations regarding the endings of your books. For example, in *Harry Potter and the Philosopher's Stone*, we see Harry vanquish Lord Voldemort temporarily, but we're made aware that this is a temporary fix and we read on to find out if the hero eventually defeats the villain for good. In romance novels, there is always the expectation of a happily ever after (HEA) or at the very least, a "happy for now" ending; however, after this ending, there is often a denouement that either introduces or reintroduces a different couple that the next book will focus on. In this case, the reader has enjoyed the complete story arc of the original couple so much that they wish to know about the next couple, therefore purchasing the next book.

The best series starters leave us satisfied but hungry for more, which means providing readers with a complete experience before pulling them into the lure of the whole series.

2. Master your pacing

The first book in your series needs to be the very best example of your work and a promise of what's to come, which means establishing a clear and even pace throughout. There's nothing worse than a book that drags from the start, or one that starts off fast but lags in the middle. Uneven pacing is a surefire way to lose readers before they've even considered the rest of your series.

Some of the most common mistakes made with the pacing of a series starter are:

1. Taking too long to introduce the cast (confession: I've made this mistake myself)
2. Info-dumping about the world for chapters on end before anything happens (most common in fantasy and sci-fi)

3. Providing too much backstory before the inciting incident

It's your job as an author to hook your reader from that very first sentence and maintain that level of intrigue throughout. If you can't master pacing in your series starter, no reader will be keen to turn to the next book. Your series starter represents what's to come, and what's to come should be an evenly paced, riveting read.

Pacing is something an author should be constantly aware of as they write and refine their manuscript. Often, newer authors assume that good pacing means *fast* pacing, which isn't always the case. Good pacing is in fact more about balance; it's about striking the right note between the action-packed scenes and the scenes that give the characters (and the reader) time to process. A trade-off between various speeds helps provide variety and keeps the narrative interesting. It's the highs and lows that keep readers intrigued; if everything is the same pace, we get bored.

Think about it – if *The Lord of the Rings* were simply battle after battle, we'd stop caring because we didn't have those quieter, slower moments of travel, of conversation around the camp where we get to know the characters. It's these varied scenes that help develop our emotional investment in the characters so that when the battles do occur, the stakes seem higher.

There are many ways you can vary the pacing throughout your books and series, such as:

- Varying the length of sentences (short for a fast pace; long for a slower pace)
- Using dialogue (short and snappy for fast-paced scenes; long and exploratory for slower-paced scenes)
- Using flashbacks

- Using inner monologue or introspection
- Increasing or decreasing the action

3. Craft relatable and compelling characters

Think about a series you love and ask yourself what drew you from one book to the next. Usually, the answer is: the characters. Readers love characters they can relate to and emotionally invest in. No one is going to read a seven-book series if they're not invested in the protagonist and their ragtag crew.

During your planning sessions, you should be building your main characters from the ground up. They need to be well-rounded, flawed and redeemable; they need to go on an inner journey in addition to the plot's journey.

What do I mean by *well-rounded*? A "round" character is one whose personality is multi-faceted and full of flaws and contradictions. They are capable of internal struggle, emotional development and depth. They also have the ability to surprise the reader. Claire Fraser from the *Outlander* series is a fantastic example of a round character. She has an intricate history and strong views that have a tendency to get her into trouble; she is bound by the oath she made as a doctor, which sees her save the lives of people many would deem unworthy of saving. Over the course of Diana Gabaldon's (so far) nine-book series, we see Claire grow and adapt in a new time period (18th century Scotland); we see her fall in love, make mistakes and experience multi-layered emotional turmoil.

Tyrion Lannister from *Game of Thrones* is another great example of a round character. As a dwarf, Tyrion faces great prejudice as well as the cruelty of his father and sister throughout his life; however, he uses his cunning and education to further his position, and we also get to see an incredibly witty side to him. He's a truly complex character who fights to achieve his own goals, all the while wrestling with his inner demons.

A flat character, on the other hand, often lacks these attributes. They can be summarised in a few words and readers are able to easily understand their role in the story. In the *Harry Potter* series, Crabbe and Goyle, Draco Malfoy's "henchmen", are solid examples of flat characters. Their roles are easily defined as the antagonist's sidekicks and they don't experience any growth or development throughout the story, and yet they contribute to the characterisation of Malfoy himself.

Over the course of your series, you will have various flat and round characters, but the takeaway here is that the main players in your cast need to feel deeply human. They need to be developed enough to sustain your readers across multiple books. If your protagonists start out flat, a reader won't continue the series.

4. Create a polished, professional product

While this book focuses on the craft of series writing, it would be remiss of me not to touch on the importance of the finished, published product. You need to offer your readers the best product possible. Remember, your series starter is a promise of what's to come, and nobody wants to wade through a messy first book just to see what happens later. Your book should showcase your knowledge of the genre and its tropes, it should meet readers' expectations, and it should certainly be professionally edited, designed and published.

5. Write the next book

As soon as you're finished with your first book, the job of the series author is always to write the next instalment. As soon as you've got your series starter as polished as possible, hand it off to your beta readers; while they're reading it and compiling their feedback, start the next manuscript. Continuing the momentum both in writing and publishing your series is the best thing you can do for your career.

TEN

Keep a Series Bible

"Creating a series bible along the way is one of the best things I did for myself and my series, but how detailed or complex you get with it is really up to your personal preference, the complexity of the series you're writing, and the amount of time you are able to put into it."
—Sarra Cannon, "How To Create A Series Bible (How To Plan & Write A Series, #4)"

ONE OF THE biggest regrets I have about *The Oremere Chronicles* is that I didn't keep a series bible while I was writing. The main trilogy consists of three books of 100,000+ words each, with four points of view and a cast of characters arguably large enough to rival that of *Game of Thrones*. It also references historical events hundreds of years in the past, spans several continents and features various types of magic. As someone whose memory isn't the strongest at the best of times, I found keeping all that information in my head incredibly challenging at the time – let alone years later, when I want to reference it in other books.

Not having a series bible led to various frustrations when I was writing the later books. I often had to go back and reread what I'd written, or ask one of my beta readers to remind me what had happened. Not exactly a streamlined process for a career author... And not exactly conducive to creating the richest, most well-rounded and consistent world, either.

After many teeth-pulling moments during the writing of the final book, *War of Mist*, I vowed that next time, it would be different. And I stuck to that promise. When I started outlining the books in the *Curse of the Cyren Queen* series, I immediately started a series bible, and it's been an absolute lifesaver ever since.

What is a series bible?

A series bible (also called a "story bible") is a document, notebook, spreadsheet or any record that an author updates and uses throughout the writing process to keep track of the various aspects of their world. The extent of the detail is entirely up to the author, but a series bible can include things such as:

- Lists of characters
- A historical timeline
- An outline of a magic system
- A hierarchy of magical creatures
- Family trees
- Settings and their attributes
- Languages
- Currencies

Why do you need a series bible?

The reasons for keeping a series bible are seemingly endless, but I'll try to keep it contained to the main ones.

. . .

Close the mental gap between books

Writing a series may span months or years of your life, and inevitably, there'll be a time where you need to take a break between writing each book. When you're not constantly immersed in your world, it can be easy to forget certain details, particularly as you get deeper into the series and it becomes more complex. Having a series bible allows you to revisit the key details of your characters and stories without having to reread the preceding books before starting the next; a refresher course, of sorts.

Track details that change across a series arc

Over the course of multiple books, settings, characters and other details may change and develop. For example, real names or lineage may be discovered; character appearances may change; new characters may be introduced... A series bible allows you to keep track of these changes and offers a point of reference for when you need to inevitably check your current work against what you've committed to in the previous books. This could be something small, like the colour of a character's eyes, or something big, like the death of a character.

Unburden your mind

As authors, we store countless concepts in our minds relevant to our stories. Usually, there's more than one narrative arc floating around in there, and it can be challenging remembering what has made it into the final manuscript and what was edited out. A series bible eases the pressure of holding all of this in your mind as you write.

. . .

Iron out inconsistencies

This is probably the main theme of the series bible: ironing out inconsistencies. A series bible is a place to store details about your setting, characters and plot, as well as timelines of events and correct spellings. Again, this saves you so much time, as you don't have to revisit multiple books to find a single detail.

Some authors utilise their series bibles even more by providing their beta readers with access so they can fact-check as they read. I personally use mine as a reference for when my audiobook publisher wants pronunciations for new character or place names in the next instalment of my series.

Tips for creating and using a series bible

My series bible started out as a blank Google Doc, which I added to every time I made a decision about my fictional world or its characters. A series bible doesn't have to be another huge task to check off your list, and it certainly doesn't have to be perfect – none of your readers are ever going to see it. The point of a series bible is to make your job easier. So let's explore how you can make it work for you...

1. Make it easy to search

The main thing you'll be doing with your series bible is using it as a point of reference. As such, you want to make it easy to search. That's why I use a working document in Google Docs and implement heading styles to generate a table of contents that's easy to navigate. For the most part, I just CTRL+F details to check, so this format suits my purpose well.

2. Make it easy to access and hard to lose

When I'm writing my manuscripts, I always have my series bible open in a new tab so I can refer to it with ease. This has been an invaluable part of my process, particularly as I become more and more immersed in the series I'm working on. Over the past few years, my series bible has evolved from a blank document to a 65-page beast of a reference book, which is why it's not only vital that it's easy for me to access (bookmarked in my browser), but that it's not easily lost. Every week, I back up my important Google Drive files both on my laptop and on a hard drive; if I were to lose my series bible at this point, it would be a disaster. This is why I suggest using a digital tool to create your own bible so you can back it up – it could be years of work in the making.

3. If you're really into notepads...

If notepads and physical records are your thing, I suggest you keep your series bible in a single notepad/folder and use colour coding, labelled sections, headings and everything you can to make things easy to find. And don't lose it. Seriously.

4. Keep it updated

Always update your series bible when you make a change in your manuscript. It should always reflect the most up-to-date/final version of your book and series. This is also why I keep my series bible open as I write – this makes it far easier to maintain its upkeep.

5. Don't go overboard

A series bible is meant to make your job easier, not add to the already huge list of tasks you need to complete. Don't fall into the trap of detailing elements you'll never explore in the series; this can become a form of procrastination. Don't spend too much time filling it out before you write – it should be a working file that gets added to, and it's fine if it starts off almost blank.

6. Include book number references

One of the best things I've done with my series bible when adding new details is referencing which book each detail is introduced in. For example, when I'm listing my cast, I'll write: *Roh/Rohesia ([F], Book 1, moss-green eyes)*; *Kezra Wisehand ([F], Book 3, aka The Carver, Arch General of Csilla)* etc. I can't tell you how many times this has made life easier for me.

7. Keep a style guide

A style guide is a little different to a whole series bible, but can be included within your series bible or as a separate document. As you write more books in the same series, you'll want to keep the styles of spellings, italics, languages and preferred punctuation consistent throughout. For example, my style guide includes details like:

- Australian spelling with *ise/ising* endings, using the *Macquarie Dictionary* as reference
- Use single quotation marks, with doubles within singles throughout
- Internal thoughts in italics
- Use open ellipses (space on either side, unless it's preceded or followed by a quotation mark)
- Use open en dash for parenthesis
- Use em dash for interruptions in text – closed if

following an incomplete word (wai—), open if
following a complete word (wait —)
- Cerys' (rather than Cerys's)
- Comma before "too" when away from the verb
- "ed" for verbs: dreamed, leaned, burned, leaned, leaped
- Towards, upwards, backwards etc. *but* forward
- Amongst/amidst
- Hyphens for compass directions i.e. south-east etc.

And…

- backahast (water horse)
- bone cleaner (only hyphenated when used adjectivally, e.g. bone-cleaner workshop)
- Bridge of Csilla

Of course, yours can be as in-depth as you like. The key is that it's easy for you to reference. A style guide is also useful when it comes to editing; you can send this aspect of your series bible to your editor to make life easier for them and to prevent them flagging deliberate choices as errors.

What software to use for your series bible

As I've mentioned above, I keep my series bible simple (and somewhat old-school) by using a Google Doc with a range of different heading styles to create a table of contents. At this stage in my career, publishing and writing are hard enough without another new learning curve. Of course, this will likely change over the next few years, as I'm always looking to improve my processes and systems – but for now, I'm happy with my current method.

There are plenty of other tools authors use successfully to keep their series bible. Some to consider:

- OneNote
- Notion
- Notes
- Scrivener
- WorldAnvil
- Hiveword
- A physical notepad and pen

What should I include in my series bible?

Often, the depth of your series bible depends on what genre you're writing in. For example, if you're writing a romance series set in a small town, your bible could consist of a list of place names and character names, along with characters' physical attributes and a family tree. If you're writing an epic fantasy saga, the world is naturally more complex and needs a lot more detail to build from scratch.

To give you an example, let's take a look at a few excerpts from my series bible for *Curse of the Cyren Queen*...

Magic system

As I'm a fantasy author, the magic system is a vital part of my series and therefore my series bible. This is a whole chunky section within my document that includes various subsections, such as:

- **Cyrens:** The creatures the whole series is based around. What are their powers? What are their distinctive traits? How long do they live? Where does cyren magic come from? Is this magic exhaustible?

- **The queen's magic:** The queen holds different magic to the regular cyrens. This is detailed here so I can recall her particular differences at a glance.
- **Water warlocks:** Creatures relevant to cyren history and the later books in the series. I detail their particular magic and traits here.
- **Sea serpents/drakes:** What are these creatures? What do they look like? Where do they live? What can they do?
- **The magic of Talon's Reach:** Talon's Reach is a setting within the books that has its own magic and character. It's enchanted so it can exist in the depths of the sea and its light mimics the natural light leagues above it.

Settings

This part of the series bible features the locations of various settings within the realm and, if needed, more in-depth descriptions for the most prominent places in the story. For example, beneath the subheading "Upper Sector" is a list of settings within this part of the lair:

- The Great Hall of Saddoriel
- The Queen's Conservatory and private gardens
- Entrance and galleries
- Upper-level outskirts of Talon's Reach
- The Vault
- The Pool of Weeping
- The Passage of Kings

- The queen's quarters

And that's just to name a few. Where a setting within this list holds crucial importance to the story or the characters, I give it its own subsection – for example, this is what I've written beneath the location "Entrance to Saddoriel":

> Entrance to the Upper Sector of Saddoriel from East Sea Underpass: Dark cavern that resembles the same wet grit of the rest of the East Sea Underpass. Sparse torchlight flickers across the walls, the light catching in the crystals of salt.
>
> A towering archway, its bright ivory tones in stark contrast to the rest of the dark cavern. It was built with … bones. Hundreds, if not thousands of bones. Loose fragments scuff underfoot.
>
> Lair wraps around the cavern in a massive circle, with numerous stone galleries that look down, seeming to stretch over a hundred feet above. Ragged stone peaks form bridges across the higher levels and in the centre of it all is a thick, rocky column that looms high: a throne.

Many settings in that initial list have their own section with a thorough description, so I can refer back to what it looks like as I write the later books and have inevitably forgotten the details.

Cyren culture

The cyrens in my series (similar to the sirens of Greek mythology) have a very rich culture with various hierarchies and rules, as well as intricate priorities and politics, so this part of my bible covers topics like:

- The Law of the Lair (far more complex than "do not murder" and "do not steal")
- Importance of music (which interlinks with history and magic)
- The Jaktaren Guild (almost a cult-like group)
- Bone architecture and building (the basis for their entire territory)

Beneath each of these subheadings is further information for my own reference. For example, under "Importance of music" I've included the following details:

- Music is the life force of the cyrens. They are sensitive to its notes and meaning
- Music plays constantly (24/7) throughout Saddoriel
- Music barely reaches the Lower Sector. They can hear faint notes, but long to hear the whole song, which makes their quality of life even crueller – the music is just out of reach
- Against the Law of the Lair for cyrens to play music; that is what humans are for. Cyrens are supposed to focus all their energies on honing their deathsong, cultivating their power from within
- Talented human musicians are still hunted and brought to the lair by the Jaktaren

Even these brief sample sections seem extensive, don't they? I assure you, my series bible looked nothing like this to begin with. As I've said, this is a living document that's constantly added to as I write. If you're interested in seeing a larger sample, I've included a link in the Bonuses section at the end of this book.

Regardless of your chosen genre, if you mean to write a successful series, I encourage you to keep a series bible. It can be much simpler than mine – for example, a list of your characters, who's related to whom and what colour eyes they have… It's completely up to you. But having a series bible will save you hours of time and frustration later, I promise.

ELEVEN

Craft a Compelling Cast of Characters

"Character evolution is at the heart of any good story. Whether it's the protagonist doing the changing, or whether he's changing the world around him, character arcs are ultimately the whole point of fiction."
—K.M. Weiland, "How To Write Character Arcs"

WHETHER YOU'RE WRITING a static or dynamic series, one of the key components of creating a stellar experience for your readers is a compelling cast of characters. It's the characters who get us to emotionally invest in the outcome of a series, and it's the characters we're cheering on as they face numerous obstacles over the course of multiple books. Readers only do this when characters are well-developed, realistic and flawed.

A great example is detective Mare Sheehan from the TV series *Mare of Easttown.* The loss of her son has made Mare closed-off and often harsh to those around her, and pressure is mounting from the year-long missing person case she is trying to solve – all of which leads to Mare making rash decisions in her personal life and being abrasive to those trying to help. These flaws and actions are all deeply human, which audiences can relate to. Mare leads a cast of complex characters, all of whom have complicated and conflicting relationships with one another. The broader plot of a murder mystery allows the development of these gripping characters to unfold.

No matter how big or small, a solid cast of characters will help sustain your series over multiple books. The beauty of a cast in a series is that they provide endless opportunities in their actions and interactions with one another.

While this chapter certainly isn't an extensive exploration of how to write compelling characters, it's my hope that it sheds some light on the roles your characters need to play throughout a series and what sort of forethought you may need as you plan.

For those who wish to study character craft in more detail, I'll list some fantastic resources at the end of this book. But for now, I want to share with you the techniques I have used to craft my own casts and what I've learned over the years.

1. Everyone has a secret and their own motivations

This is my first port of call when it comes to creating characters for my series. Secrets make for utterly compelling character arcs because eventually, they'll be found out. Secrets have a way of being uncovered and always have the power to turn the tides of a conflict.

The same goes for character motivations – every significant player in your series should have their own motivations that inform their actions. What is at stake for them? What do they hope to gain? For example…

- Katniss Everdeen wants to protect her sister Prim from the Hunger Games. Her life is at stake, but she hopes her actions will save her sister
- Daphne Bridgerton wants to find a suitable husband.

Her reputation and her family's reputation are at stake. She hopes to gain a family of her own and a high place in society
- Frodo wants to destroy the One Ring and protect the Shire and Middle-earth. His life and the fate of his entire world is at stake. He hopes for peace and the survival of his home

2. Understand character archetypes and roles

Every character should have a primary thematic force or role to play. It's the author's job to identify these roles and develop them further. If you're stumped as to what sort of characters to include, you may want to explore various archetypes as inspiration for your own ideas. There are dozens upon dozens of books about character archetypes, but the most commonly referenced archetypes are as follows:

- Protagonist – like Katniss Everdeen, Daphne Bridgerton, Frodo Baggins
- Antagonist – like President Snow, Lord Nigel Berbrooke, Sauron
- Sidekick – like Gale Hawthorne (also a potential love interest), Penelope Featherington, Samwise Gamgee
- Mentor or guardian – like Haymitch Abernathy, Lady Danbury, Gandalf
- Love interest – like Peeta Mellark, Simon Basset, Arwen

Take some time to identify each character's role, both in terms of the individual books and the series as a whole. Ask yourself: what do they contribute to the eventual payoff of the series ending?

Let's look at some of the *Hunger Games* examples from above. Katniss, President Snow, Gale, Haymitch and Peeta all have a direct impact on the plot. Katniss kickstarts the entire narrative with her choice to "volunteer as tribute" in the place of her sister, and her development over the course of the series incites an entire uprising against the Capitol and the eventual end of the Hunger Games.

President Snow's goals of keeping Panem under his control and ending Katniss' legacy cause a knock-on effect that unites the people and sparks a rebellion that changes the course of history.

Katniss' friendship with Gale helps her develop the skills she uses to survive the Hunger Games. He is also a vocal rebel, whose ideas eventually influence Katniss' own perception of the rebellion.

As a previous victor of the Hunger Games, Haymitch's experience and cunning helps guide Katniss and Peeta through the trials.

Peeta's contribution starts by defying the rule that the Games can only have one winner, which in turn incites the broader rebellion against the Capitol.

Characters who don't affect the story should be cut – everyone should serve a purpose, even if it's only a small one.

3. Decide on the type of character arc

Over the course of your series, your characters will go through various arcs of change and development – inner journeys, if you like. More often than not, these arcs fall into one of three categories:

- Change/transformation arc
- Growth arc

- Fall/negative arc

Let's briefly explore these...

Change/transformation arc

Most transformation or change arcs involve the character in question (usually the protagonist) believing a misconception about themselves or the world. The character then discovers the truth; the way they react to this, and how they transform in the face of it, forms the foundation of their character arc.

A clear example of the change arc is Harry Potter, who believes that he is just an ordinary kid until he discovers the truth: that he's a wizard. This sets his whole character arc in motion and his transformation from ordinary boy to the courageous wizard who eventually saves the world from Lord Voldemort.

If you choose the change/transformation arc for your characters, you need to ask yourself: what do they believe that's false? How do they uncover the truth? And how does this track over the course of your series? Perhaps your characters have more than one change arc, or perhaps it's slow to unfold, taking multiple books to be revealed... Who will your characters be at the end of the transformation arc?

Growth arc

Slightly different to the arc listed above, a growth arc is when a character overcomes something within themselves, but it doesn't necessarily change them as a person. This can mean learning something new, changing their perspective on a particular issue, or changing roles by the end of the arc.

A good example of this is Geralt of Rivia from *The Witcher*.

Geralt is a gruff monster hunter who doesn't want any friends; it's not until the protection of Princess Cirilla is forced upon him that we see a completely different side to Geralt – a paternal side. We see him grow from being concerned only about himself and his next payment to being a guardian and father figure to a vulnerable young girl.

When creating a growth arc, ask yourself: what has my character learned? Have they improved themselves? Are they different to the character who was introduced at the start of the series? As with the previous arc, you should map this out across the span of your books.

Fall/negative arc

This type of character arc is the one that usually results in a character's fall from grace due to poor choices they've made. This arc is most commonly used for the villains of stories, to explain their motivations and to create intrigue surrounding why they are the way they are. A strong example of a negative arc is the corruption of Anakin Skywalker in *Star Wars*, where he undergoes a transformation from an idealistic young man to the infamous villain, Darth Vader.

4. Everyone has flaws and emotional wounds

If you want to hold a reader's attention for three or more books, the last thing you want is a perfect character. Some newer writers have a tendency to make their protagonists good-looking, talented, popular and everything in between, which often results in a dull cardboard cut-out of a character.

After reading a book where the protagonist makes no mistakes and incites no conflict, will a reader really want to keep going? No. Readers want characters who are complicated, flawed and contrary, just as people are in real life. They want to see negative traits as much as positive ones, and more than anything, they want to be able to relate to the characters.

Thus, it's an author's responsibility to ensure that their characters have flaws (negative traits), as well as emotional wounds: "A negative experience (or set of experiences) that causes pain on a deep psychological level. It is a lasting hurt that often involves someone close... Wounds may be tied to a specific event, arise upon learning a difficult truth about the world, or result from a physical limitation, condition or challenge." (Becca Puglisi and Angela Ackerman, *The Emotional Wound Thesaurus: A Writer's Guide to Psychological Trauma*)

Before I start my series, I like to sit down and brainstorm numerous character traits, flaws and emotional wounds, determining which might serve my main character and contribute to the arc of the series.

5. Map out relationship arcs

Don't just look at your main handful of characters – take the top 10 or more and study how they interact with one another. What are their relationships? Who is hiding something from someone? Who is the peacekeeper? Who's the troublemaker? Neutral characters make for a boring story.

Think back to your favourite series. Which characters have the most intriguing dynamic? Why? Is this something you can use to generate your own ideas? Think about your own friends and family. There are natural leaders and followers, extroverts and introverts – how do they all interact?

The beauty of a series is that you have time to develop and change the relationships of your characters over the course of several books. For example, Legolas and Gimli from *The Lord of the Rings* start out as enemies and gradually become friends; by the end of the epic quest, they're ride-or-die. In *Bridgerton*, our lead Daphne originally hates the arrogant Duke of Hastings, but over the course of the season, their relationship develops from one of mutual convenience to one of friendship and, eventually, love.

In real life, relationships are ever-changing and unpredictable, and so it should be in fiction as well. Those who started out as enemies can become lovers; those who started out as friends can become rivals; friendships can be solidified or they can fall apart; family can become estranged just as easily as new members can be welcomed into the fold. The point is that your characters' relationships with one another should change and evolve throughout your series.

6. Don't introduce everyone all at once

Series tend to have much bigger casts than standalone novels, but that doesn't mean you need to introduce everyone at the same time. This will only overwhelm your readers and frustrate them when they can't remember who's who. Writing a series gives you the luxury of time – you can afford to introduce new characters in the later books, once your readers are familiar with the main cast.

7. Create character profiles

Another technique some writers use to develop their cast is creating character profiles. This involves filling out a questionnaire of sorts that summarises various details about that character. It can include things like eye colour, hair colour, height, interests, whether or not they completed school, what they're afraid of, and so on. You can find an array of templates online, or you can simply make your own. How granular you go is completely up to you. Personally, I'm usually satisfied with a brief physical description and then more information about their personality and motivations, which I include in my series bible.

8. Layer in character detail post-first draft and make notes for future books

My first drafts tend to be quite skeletal. That initial "skinny" draft is usually about the physical logistics of the plot: where the book is set, where the characters go and why. If I don't lay the foundation down first, I can get easily overwhelmed by the scope of all I have to include. So one way I combat this is by making note of the character arcs and details I want to include in the series and in each book, and once the first draft is done, I go back with a character focus and layer these details in. As I do this, I also make note of what I need to reference in the books to come, and the open character arcs that will need to be addressed later in the series.

For example, in my *Curse of the Cyren Queen* series, my protagonist Roh has a talent for architectural sketches. I decided that this would be a character trait of hers: that sketching is something she uses to clear her mind when she's anxious. So, throughout the reworking stage of each book, I went back over the manuscripts to layer this detail in. I added scenes where she was sketching, scenes where she wished she could be sketching, sentences where she noticed a unique architectural detail and a scene where her love interest gave her a new sketchpad.

Final character pointers

- Group similar characters – you may find instances where you need a lot of bodies in the room, but you don't need to name every single minor character there. Group them together and give them a spokesperson who can represent them all. It will save you a lot of additional, unnecessary work, and will save your reader a lot of confusion

- Don't get bogged down in physical descriptions of your characters – leave some things up to the reader and their imagination

- My general rule is that unless a character has a prolonged speaking role or significant part to play in the narrative, they shouldn't even be named. There's nothing worse than a reader trying to remember 40 names of unimportant minor characters

- Use your series bible to keep track of your cast! Every time I add to the cast, I add the name of the character and a few brief details to my series bible

- Keep an eye on your protagonist – sometimes when we write an ensemble cast, an author can fall for one of the secondary characters, putting more effort into *their* characterisation than that of the protagonist. Your protagonist should always be the driving force of the narrative

- Don't default to passivity – another common mistake I see newer authors make is having a bunch of things happen *to* their protagonist, rather than their protagonist making choices of their own that drive the narrative forward through the series

TWELVE

Use Foreshadowing and Breadcrumbs

"Foreshadowing is a key tool for writers to build dramatic tension and suspense throughout their stories. Foreshadowing makes your reader wonder what will happen next, and keeps them reading to find out."
—"Writing 101: Foreshadowing Definition, Examples of Foreshadowing, and How to Use Foreshadowing in Your Writing" (MasterClass.com)

WHAT DRAWS readers from one chapter to the next? And from one book in a series to the sequel? And the next book? And the next? At the core of every reader's motivation for reading is that there's something they want to know, and it's the author's job to fuel this drive with unanswered questions, clues and hints at a future to come.

So how do we build and maintain this intrigue not just over the course of a single book, but an entire series? How does an author propel a narrative forward and lead the reader through the story? How can we build up to the reveals and ultimately cement the payoff for the reader? How do we create the "Aha!"

moment, where pieces of the puzzle fall into place and it all makes sense? How can we make the reader understand the plot in hindsight with appreciation, rather than frustration at the predictability? How can we create plausibility within our stories?

The answer: we can use foreshadowing and breadcrumbs.

Foreshadowing

Foreshadowing is a literary device used to create a hint or warning of what's to come throughout the story. It creates intrigue, dramatic suspense and tension that draws a reader in, piquing their curiosity and driving them to read on. More often than not, foreshadowing has negative or ominous connotations, hinting at darker conflicts to come.

Examples of foreshadowing in literature can generally be split into two categories: direct and indirect.

Direct foreshadowing

This type of foreshadowing is a straightforward prediction or statement that sets the reader's expectation of what's to come.

Let's use *Harry Potter* as our example. In Chapter One of J.K. Rowling's *Harry Potter and the Philosopher's Stone*, Professor McGonagall says to Dumbledore: "He'll be famous – a legend – I wouldn't be surprised if today was known as Harry Potter day in the future – there will be books written about Harry – every child in our world will know his name!"

This is direct foreshadowing at its best, as the reader discovers that Harry is indeed famous in the following chapters, set 10 years later; when Harry visits Diagon Alley with Hagrid, strangers shake his hand and know his name. It also foreshadows that Harry's story is far from over and that by the end of the series, he will be even more famous than before.

Another example is the conversation that takes place between Frodo and Gandalf in the film version of *The Fellowship of the Ring*:

FRODO: It's a pity Bilbo didn't kill [Gollum] when he had the chance.

GANDALF: Pity? It was pity that stayed Bilbo's hand. Many that die deserve life, and some that live deserve death. Can you give it to them, Frodo? Do not be too eager to deal out death in judgement. Even the very wise cannot see all ends. My heart tells me that Gollum has some part to play, for good or ill, before this is over. The pity of Bilbo may rule the fate of many.

In the next instalments of the series, *The Two Towers* and *The Return of the King*, we discover that Gandalf was indeed right – it is Gollum who leads Frodo and Sam to Mordor to destroy the One Ring, thus acting as the driving force for the whole narrative.

Indirect foreshadowing

Indirect foreshadowing is less obvious. This device uses subtle hints and suggestions at what's to come; more often than not, a reader doesn't understand the significance of these clues until the main reveal has happened. Indirect foreshadowing can be presented as motifs, symbols, metaphors and subtext.

One example is the repetition of the motto of House Stark, "Winter is coming", in the *Game of Thrones* TV adaptation. This is a brilliant piece of indirect foreshadowing, as it actually has three meanings. The first is a more general "hard times are coming" warning, but the second pertains to the overarching plot of the entire series: the impending battle between the White Walkers and humankind. Thirdly, it acts as a metaphor for the Starks themselves – specifically when Arya Stark kills the Frey household, telling the survivors, "Winter came for House Frey".

Breadcrumbs

Truth be told, I could have included the concept of "breadcrumbs" under the umbrella of foreshadowing, because breadcrumbs are like its younger, happier cousin. However, I think they deserve their own subsection for a few reasons – chiefly that a breadcrumb can be as minor or major as the author sees fit.

Where foreshadowing is typically more ominous and big-picture, breadcrumbs are clues of varying significance pertaining to reveals of varying size that will happen throughout the series. Not only do breadcrumbs help propel the narrative forward, they are also used to *reward the reader* for paying attention, offering smaller, more regular instances of that much sought-after "payoff" to sustain a reader over the course of multiple books. The very term "breadcrumb" is a reference to the story of Hansel and Gretel, where the siblings leave a trail of breadcrumbs to help them find their way. This is exactly what an author does for their readers.

One of my favourite examples of a perfectly executed breadcrumb is from *Avengers: Age of Ultron*. It's a seemingly small moment where our heroes are all gathered in the Avengers complex, a tad tipsy, taking turns at trying to lift Thor's hammer (which only Thor has the power to do). After several failed attempts, we get to Captain America's turn. The camera shows

Thor's face, which subtly suggests he thinks Cap might be able to lift it. We see Cap try, and the hammer moves ever so slightly – or does it? It's so quick, so subtle that the viewer is left questioning if we even saw it. This scene is then ostensibly forgotten about in the 10 MCU films between that moment and *Avengers: Endgame*. In the final battle, while Thor is at the mercy of the villain Thanos, we are shown a close-up of his hammer being picked up by someone else… And that someone turns out to be Captain America, followed by Thor saying, "I knew it!". For those who noticed the breadcrumb all the way back in *Age of Ultron*, this payoff is far more impactful.

Ways to include foreshadowing and breadcrumbs

1. Use dialogue

An author can use dialogue to foreshadow directly or indirectly. It can be something as obvious as one character saying to another, "I've got a bad feeling about this," which is used in numerous films, TV shows and books, to something a little more abstract, like the following from *Game of Thrones*: "People die at their dinner tables. They die in their beds. They die squatting over their chamber pots. Everybody dies sooner or later. And don't worry about your death. Worry about your life. Take charge of your life for as long as it lasts." (David Benioff & D. B. Weiss, "The Mountain and the Viper")

From the outset, this could be construed as simple life advice from Littlefinger to Robin Arryn; however, this single quote ultimately foreshadows three major deaths: Joffrey Baratheon (poisoned at his wedding feast), Tyrion Lannister's lover Shae (strangled to death in her bed), and Tyrion's father Tywin (shot with a crossbow while on the toilet).

We can find a similar example in *Star Wars: Episode II*, when

Obi-Wan Kenobi says to Anakin Skywalker: "Why do I get the feeling you will be the death of me?" This question echoes in the viewer's mind when later, Anakin-turned-Darth Vader does indeed kill Obi-Wan.

2. Use symbolism

Symbolism is a common literary device where the author uses a symbol to represent something beyond the literal meaning. This could be anything: an object, the weather, locations, clothing, colours, even a character's actions, as long as it's used in a way that evokes additional meaning or emotion. Symbolism can be an impactful tool for creating powerful indirect foreshadowing and effective breadcrumbs.

A simple example would be describing a change to foul weather in order to create a foreboding mood and tone to start a scene, such as storm clouds looming overhead.

A more sophisticated example would be the orphaned direwolf pups in the first season of *Game of Thrones*. The mother wolf has been killed by a stag, foreshadowing that the Stark children will eventually be orphaned when Ned and Catelyn Stark die. It also foreshadows the way that the Baratheon (stag sigil) and Stark (direwolf sigil)'s fates are entwined.

3. Name but don't explain

This is where the author refers to something by name, but doesn't explain what it is. The reader is left wondering what role this particular thing will play over the course of the book.

Take this example from *The Hunger Games*: "When I wake up, the other side of the bed is cold. My fingers stretch out, seeking Prim's warmth but finding only the rough canvas cover of the mattress. She must have had bad dreams and climbed in with our mother. Of course, she did. This is the day of the reaping."

Here, Suzanne Collins draws the reader's attention to something foreboding called "the reaping", but doesn't go on to explain what this event is. All the reader knows is that it's something *bad*, bad enough to invoke nightmares that might make a person crawl into bed with their mother.

I do something similar throughout my *Curse of the Cyren Queen* series by referring to shameful events in cyren history: the Age of Chaos and the Scouring of Lochloria. It's only as the reader continues through the series that they come to understand the full scale of horror these events entail.

4. Use the narrator

Whether you're using first or third person, the narrator can often be utilised to implement effective foreshadowing. In Robin Hobb's series, *The Farseer Trilogy*, the narrator is the protagonist, Fitz, when he is much older, looking back to his younger self and earlier years. In the prologue of *Assassin's Apprentice*, he speaks of his first love, Molly: "Of my magics and my other profession, she knew nothing. Maybe that was why I could love her. It was certainly why I lost her..."

The narrator is foreshadowing one of the key events in his life. Although the reader is not yet told how, we are suddenly aware of what's to come: heartbreak for our hero.

5. Put it in the title

Foreshadowing doesn't only take place within the books themselves, but can also be used in the titles of individual volumes in order to make a promise to the reader. For example:

- *The Return of Sherlock Holmes*
- *The Return of the King*
- *Murder on the Orient Express*

If it suits your genre and writing style, you also have the option to include a hint of foreshadowing in chapter titles. Patrick Rothfuss uses this to great effect throughout the *Kingkiller Chronicle* books – just look at the following titles from *The Name of the Wind*:

- "A Place for Demons"
- "The Price of Remembering"
- "A Parting of Ways"

Tips for creating effective foreshadowing and breadcrumbs

- Read widely in your chosen genre and be on the lookout for examples of these techniques done well
- Be mindful of finding the balance between not enough foreshadowing and too much. You don't want the reader to guess the ending straight away, nor do you want the ending to come out of nowhere and seem unbelievable
- Refer to your overarching series plan and note down details that need to be threaded throughout each individual book
- Don't try to achieve all your foreshadowing while writing your first drafts; it can be layered in during the editing stage
- Get feedback from beta readers as to whether or not your foreshadowing and breadcrumbs are effective
- Often foreshadowing occurs at the beginning of a

story, but as you're writing a series, be sure to weave it consistently throughout the series arc as a whole

- If you're going to use foreshadowing and breadcrumbs, don't forget about them! Never leave them unfulfilled – this is a common error to make, particularly when writing in series, so keep track of your breadcrumbs and foreshadowing in your series bible

THIRTEEN

Use Open Loops and Cliffhangers

"Writing a series is a challenging dichotomy. You want to create satisfying and complete novels, yet the novels contain threads to pull the reader from book to book. It's a balancing act."
—Sara Rosett, *How to Write A Series*

FOR A SERIES TO be called a "page turner", "unputdownable" and "addictive", there must always be larger forces at play... And by that I mean savvy authors using open loops and cliffhangers to maintain reader intrigue and investment in a series. Used alongside foreshadowing and breadcrumbs, these techniques have the power to create that overwhelming need to read "just one more chapter" or one-click-buy that next book... The reader needs to know what happens next!

Open loops and cliffhangers can be used side by side over the course of a series, and both techniques can bridge the gap between both chapters and books. Like foreshadowing, these methods build momentum and drive characters and readers forward through the narrative. But what are they, exactly, and how do they achieve this?

Open loops

An open loop is a story arc that's initially open-ended or unresolved, which can take the form of subplots or something more minor. These are not as high-stakes as cliffhangers (which we'll get to shortly), but serve the same purpose of piquing the reader's curiosity, making them wonder what happens next and driving them to read on, from chapter to chapter and book to book. Funnily enough, the term "open loop" is actually more commonly used in the marketing and copywriting industry, but the purpose is the same in fiction: to grab a reader's attention and sustain it.

Open loops can be created in three main ways: by asking a question, by the discovery of a clue or by investigating something.

Asking questions

A great example of an open loop that asks a question is in *Gossip Girl* (both the TV show and books), where the overarching question is: "Who is Gossip Girl?" While the episodes and books follow the cast of rich teenagers throughout the dramas of their lives, the open loop that pulls the audience through the whole series is whether or not they'll discover Gossip Girl's secret identity. Who is the person who has shared the intimate happenings of the characters' lives? Who is responsible for so much of the drama? A similar question is woven throughout the *Bridgerton* series: "Who is Lady Whistledown?" These questions act as a common thread that tie all the books and episodes together.

Discovering a clue

Clues aren't just for mysteries and crime thrillers – they can be planted throughout a series of any genre to lead a reader from one book to the next. For example, in Sarah J. Maas' popular series opener, *Throne of Glass*, we're introduced to a world where magic has been destroyed. However, early in the book, protagonist Celaena discovers strange evidence upon waking: "Small white flowers lay at the foot of her cot, and many infant-sized footprints led in and out of the tent. Before someone could enter and notice, Celaena swept a foot over the tracks, destroying any trace, and stuffed the flowers into a nearby satchel." This is the first clue the reader receives that hints at the fact that magic might not have been as thoroughly removed from the realms as the king would have us believe. This small moment acts as a clue towards not only the eventual return of magic to the world over the course of the next few books, but to Celaena's reveal as a creature of magic herself.

Investigating something

Again, this type of open loop is not restricted to the crime or mystery genres. It could involve a character investigating their heritage, seeking the truth about a particular event in history, or looking into a ring of traitors. It simply involves the uncovering of a truth.

———

Often, open loops can combine or fall into more than one of the above categories, but ultimately they all follow their own mini arc of rising action, climax and denouement. These can be woven throughout a single chapter, a whole book, or better still, an entire series, always adding to the suspense and anticipation of the narrative arc, sometimes interlinking with one another. In any given series there can be dozens of open loops in progress, each at different stages of development/discovery to the reader.

I've used open loops to this effect throughout my own work. In the *Curse of the Cyren Queen* quartet, I use the prologue of each title to address the ongoing question of why the protagonist's mother is in prison and what really went on the day she became the infamous criminal she's now known to be. As we progress through the prologues of each book, we learn more and more about this character, before finally, in the third act of the last book, the truth is revealed and this open loop is closed.

Cliffhangers

The term "cliffhanger" is generally thought to have originated around the time the serialised version of Thomas Hardy's novel, *A Pair of Blue Eyes,* was published in *Tinsley's Magazine.* At the end of this story, one of the protagonists, Henry Knight, is left hanging off a cliff, literally.

Of course, cliffhangers don't always have to be this literal. Now, they're understood as an unexpected plot twist that usually occurs at the end of a series instalment, be it books, TV or film. They usually fall into one or more of the following categories:

- A shocking revelation (e.g. a great loss; unexpected news)
- A crucial choice (e.g. deciding between two loves; weighing up a decision for the greater good)
- An unanswered question (e.g. will the protagonist survive? What will be the state of the world?)

All three are endings that "leave you hanging" at the moment of climax. Readers and viewers often have a love–hate relationship with this device. While it leaves us wanting more, it can also be incredibly unsatisfying, especially if you've invested hours or even years of your life in following the story. As Crista Rucker says in the article "Keys to Great Endings": "... the ending is the last chance you have to impress your reader before they pick up your next book. Do you want to wow them or [leave] them feeling dissatisfied?"

Arguably, the effectiveness and/or satisfaction of using cliffhangers like these can also come down to an author's release schedule. If an author is rapid releasing (for example, publishing once a month), fans may be more forgiving when it comes to getting closure – and as for a series that's completely published, it's actually the fastest track to a one-click buy.

However, it's this fear of disappointing readers that prompts many authors to split their cliffhangers into the following categories: hard cliffhangers and soft cliffhangers.

Hard cliffhangers

Whether we've experienced it ourselves or have heard about the table-flipping from readers, we all know the power that cliffhangers can have. For authors, this can be a good or a bad thing. It's all well and good to leave readers wanting more, but do we really want to leave them with their hands thrust into the air, rage on their face, shouting, "How can it just end like that?!"

More often than not, these types of "hard" cliffhanger endings are unsatisfying and leave the reader feeling cheated because the story arc is incomplete. After all, they just spent hours, if not days reading the book, only to have it end abruptly without a decent explanation, and readers like to feel a book is worth their investment of time.

However, a hard cliffhanger often leaves a reader momentarily stunned by the fact that after all the protagonist has been through, before they can triumph over that final hurdle, the story simply ends.

The fifth novel of George R.R. Martin's *A Song of Ice and Fire* series, *A Dance with Dragons*, is a great example of both a shocking revelation and an unanswered question. The last point-of-view chapter from much-loved character Jon Snow ends with this: "Jon fell to his knees. He found the dagger's hilt and wrenched it free. In the cold night air the wound was smoking. 'Ghost,' he whispered. Pain washed over him. *Stick them with the pointy end.* When the third dagger took him between the shoulder blades, he gave a grunt and fell face-first into the snow. He never felt the fourth knife. Only the cold..."

The reader is left wondering how, if at all, Jon Snow will survive this attack. To make matters even more intense, this instalment was published in 2011, and at the time of writing this book in 2022, the release date for the sequel has yet to be announced. Readers (those who've avoided the TV adaptation, at least) have been waiting over a decade to learn Jon Snow's fate.

Another fantastic example is the ending of the film *Avengers: Infinity War*, where during the final battle, Thanos dons the completed Infinity Gauntlet, snaps his fingers and wipes out half of all life in the universe. In a prolonged sequence, we see many of our favourite characters from the franchise disintegrate to ash. Viewers are left gaping in disbelief that Marvel would kill off so many popular superheroes in one fell swoop.

An example of this from my own work is the ending of my novel, *Heart of Mist*, wherein the main character, Bleak, has just escaped from capture and a horrific fate, only to face mist she knows to be deadly:

She hauled the wheel right, veering *Arden's Fortune* away from Moredon Tower. And there, just south of the tower, was not land, but mist.

Bleak straightened herself; she wasn't going to die for the king. She wasn't going to become a prisoner or experiment of his. She'd rather die with salt water in her lungs and mist in her heart. She was free. She had to try.

Steadying the wheel, the ship lurched forward. Bleak took a deep breath, and let the waves of mist rush in around her.

The reader is left wondering what became of Bleak – did the deadly mist kill her? Or is there something we don't know? I should add that it was over a year until the sequel *Reign of Mist* was released, though I employed strategies to keep my readers satisfied between books (which we'll explore later).

Soft cliffhangers

A "soft" cliffhanger ensures that the main arc of the story is complete, but creates a new open loop or inciting incident at the end to pique the reader's curiosity about what happens next. It is a far less abrupt way to get your reader turning to the next book in your series, ensuring that while they are satisfied with the arc of the current book, they're lured to the call of adventure in the next.

A strong example of the use of a soft cliffhanger is in the Netflix series *Bridgerton*. In the last episode of season one, all is well with our main couple, Daphne and Simon, and they welcome a baby boy into the world after several episodes of romantic turmoil. However, in the final moments of the episode, we are shown Daphne's brother, Anthony Bridgerton, who has been something of a wayward soul in the first season, vowing to find himself a sensible match but eliminate love from the equation, thus setting up the main arc of the next season. The books by Julia Quinn follow the same pattern of using soft cliffhangers at the end of each volume to introduce the romantic arc of the following book.

I have also employed the soft cliffhanger strategy at the end of my series starter, *A Lair of Bones*. Throughout the book, the protagonist, Roh, has faced the challenges of a deadly tournament, from which she emerges victorious. However, a spanner is thrown in the works by a technicality, and we learn that the story is only just beginning:

> When she reached the mouth of the cave, she nearly cried out at what lay beyond. She didn't need to look at the map she carried to know where they were. They had made it. They were exactly where they ought to be: at the very beginning.
>
> She lifted a foot and made to step forward, rigid, waiting for the tether to snap in place, waiting for her freedom to be leashed —
>
> Smooth, black pebbles crunched beneath her boot.
>
> The threshold between her realm and Odi's was behind her. A stony shore greeted her with a breeze that tasted of salt and whipped through her hair.
>
> Rohesia the bone cleaner breathed it in deeply. With her band of unlikely companions at her back, she stepped into the new world that beckoned.

While the reader (hopefully) feels satisfied that the story arc of the initial tournament has come to a close, the promise of new adventure acts as an invitation, encouraging the reader to go straight to the next book in the series.

Tips for writing effective cliffhangers

1. Lay the groundwork

Remember all that planning and foreshadowing we discussed earlier? These are the techniques an author must use to lay the groundwork of the narrative in the build-up to using a cliffhanger. The story should progress logically, with peaks and troughs of conflict and resolution, slowly building to the end. Without this groundwork, a cliffhanger ending will seem tacked on and unnecessary, with the risk of the reader not even caring.

2. Only use soft cliffhangers for the end of the first book in a series

Personally, I'd recommend soft cliffhangers for the endings of most books, no matter where they fit in the series, in order to avoid unhappy readers (unless you're releasing quickly). Hard cliffhangers are great for chapter endings and for getting the reader to turn pages in a frenzy, but this style can be risky for the end of an entire book – particularly the first book in a series, where you're still gaining the reader's trust and trying to hook them into the time-heavy (and sometimes costly) commitment of reading multiple books. You don't want to leave them feeling cheated at the end of book one. You need to give them a complete experience here, before luring them into the next volume with the promise of more adventure.

3. Continue the momentum

Whether you use a hard or soft cliffhanger, you need to continue that momentum in the next instalment. There's nothing more disappointing than reading a heart-pounding cliffhanger only for the story to fall flat in the next book. You need to reward the reader for continuing with the series and ensure that cliffhanger was warranted.

4. Don't use a cliffhanger at the end of a series

Can you think of anything worse than investing time and money in a lengthy series, only to have it end with no resolution? Don't do that to your readers. Ending a series on a cliffhanger is a surefire way to stall your career.

FOURTEEN

Write Nail-Biting Sequels and Later Books

"Identify what made the first book special, then offer more."
—Brent Hartinger, "Writing Sequels: 7 Rules for Writing Second Installments"

AS SOON AS you're finished with your first book, the job of the series author is always to write the next volume. However, sequels and later books often have a poor reputation for being worse than their predecessors. Through my research, it became clear to me that this is at the forefront of many authors' minds, as some of the most commonly asked questions were: "How do I sustain reader interest over the course of several books?" and "How do I write a better sequel?" In addition to the elements we've already covered, here's how to up the ante with the books that follow your series starter...

1. Know how much to recap and where to start the story

We've all read those sequels that either insist on dragging us through 10 pages of summarised events before the action starts, or start so far after the events of the previous book that we feel lost.

There are a handful of options when it comes to recapping previous book/s for your readers. Some authors include a brief section prior to the book's main content titled "Previously", which acts as a short summary of the previous book's main plot points. Fellow indie author Sarah K.L. Wilson does this in her *Empire of War & Wings* series – you can actually see an example if you view the "Look Inside" feature of books two to five on Amazon.

Jay Kristoff approaches this in a different way with *Godsgrave*, the sequel to *Nevernight*. Before the story starts, he includes a brief section titled "Dramatis Personae" (a character list most commonly utilised at the beginning of a dramatic work), where he not only lists the main players in his book, but where they're at in the narrative. For example: "**Mister Kindly** – a daemon … made of shadows, who eats Mia's fear. He saved her life as a child, and claims to know very little about his true nature, though he's been known to lie from time to time …"

Kristoff lists names and brief summaries for 29 characters in this section, allowing his readers to recall the relevant details of the previous book before diving into the next one.

Another alternative is to include subtle reminders within the following book's opening chapters. This is the most commonly used option in series and the one I chose to utilise in *Curse of the Cyren Queen*. For example, in Chapter One of the second book, *With Dagger and Song*: "Roh couldn't be sure how far they'd journeyed since crossing the threshold of the cyren territory of Talon's Reach into the lands above almost two weeks ago."

In this single sentence, we are reminded that the protagonist, Roh, and her band of companions have left Talon's Reach, crossing the border into another territory. We are also given an indicator of how much time has passed between the end of the last book and the beginning of this book. I decided my readers probably didn't need to read several chapters of the characters' monotonous journey, and so skipped ahead to the start of the action.

Whichever option you prefer, a brief recap or subtle reminders are important to include, especially if you're leaving months or years between releases. You can't expect readers to remember every detail of the previous book without some sort of hint to jumpstart their memory.

A gripping sequel still needs to drop the reader right into the action with an inciting incident. Knowing where to start your following books is often about achieving a fine balance between action and exposition. Though most readers like to pick up right where they left off in the previous book, as the author, it's completely up to you to determine how much time has passed between volumes – it just needs to be made clear.

2. Offer a complete arc (again)

We touched on the inciting incident above, but your sequels and later books should also contain a midpoint and climax to achieve a complete narrative arc of their own. A good sequel still offers the reader a complete experience, which also helps avoid the dreaded "middle book syndrome". This is where many follow-up books go wrong and don't live up to the quality of their predecessors.

3. Challenge the "rules" and expectations

It can be easy to fall into a pattern of predictability when writing series, so one of the best things you can do to ensure your readers remain enraptured is to challenge their expectations. J.K. Rowling does this well in the final Harry Potter book, *Harry Potter in the Deathly Hallows.* For six books prior, a pattern of going to Hogwarts has been established; the reader knows that in each book, we experience a full school year. However, in the final book, our three heroes *don't* return to the wizarding school – instead they go on the run, trying to find the remaining Horcruxes all over the country.

My *Curse of the Cyren Queen* series sets up a formula of facing a challenge and obtaining a magic gem in books two, three and four. However, *The Fabric of Chaos* challenges this when Roh fails to get the gem, thus failing the quest in the middle of book three – unexpected!

Dismantle the ideas you introduced in book one (and earlier books if you're deeper into your series). Does the villain become the hero, like Snape in *Harry Potter*? Does the hero fall from grace, like Anakin Skywalker in *Star Wars*? Think about what the reader expects and see if you can turn those expectations on their heads.

4. Progression of character arcs

Remember those character arcs we've been setting up and planning for? The later books in your series are where you start to explore how your characters change, struggle and grow from who they were in book one. Ask yourself: what new obstacles do they face? How do these impact their personality and their actions? Even with a static series like *Sherlock Holmes*, the character faces new challenges that test him.

Your characters and their relationships with one another should continue to develop throughout your series. Friendships can blossom or fall apart, unexpected romances can spark, truths can be revealed about the protagonist's true heritage... There's no limit to how things can unfold.

Test your characters and their relationships with new

challenges and obstacles; this keeps the tension high and the readers turning the pages. You can also utilise secondary characters who previously had minor roles to fulfil a different purpose in later books. Alternatively, if an old character serves no purpose any longer, give them a reason to leave.

5. Know what readers loved about the first book and give them more, but with a twist

As you're working on the sequel and later books in your series, you should have some form of feedback about the first book, be it beta reader feedback or early reviews. Identify what people loved about that first instalment and make sure to include this again in the following volumes, only ramp it up – give them more, but with a twist.

For example, everyone loved the nail-biting events of *The Hunger Games*, so author Suzanne Collins included them again in the sequel, *Catching Fire*. Only she knew she couldn't just copy and paste the exact same tournament and risk losing fans to boredom. Instead, she put a twist on the Hunger Games: all the competitors this time around were winners of previous Games. Clever, right?

J.K. Rowling does a similar thing throughout the *Harry Potter* series, where each year we return to Hogwarts but face new challenges – like the Chamber of Secrets opening, the Dementors guarding the school, the Triwizard Tournament and so forth.

6. Raise the stakes or make them different

One common mistake I see authors committing is making the stakes too high from the very beginning of their series. The rest of their books then fall flat because there's seemingly no way to ramp the stakes up even further.

This is where all that planning comes into play. Each book should raise the stakes and make the story arc all the more gripping. If the stakes can't go any higher, make them different. Perhaps something else entirely is at risk?

Some things to consider when raising or changing the stakes of the story within your series:

- Every action has a consequence, even victories
- What do your characters stand to gain or lose in the face of each challenge?
- Is there a ticking clock putting pressure on your cast?
- Return to your characters' motives – what will happen if they don't achieve their goals?

7. Introduce new characters

Another way to keep a series interesting is to introduce new characters. Just as people come and go in real life, so should characters in your series. New characters can breathe new life into a story by challenging the existing characters and changing the dynamic of your current cast.

Think about your favourite series and your favourite characters within them. When were they introduced? For me, it's Sirius Black, who wasn't introduced until book three in the *Harry Potter* series. Similarly, in the *Throne of Glass* series by Sarah J. Maas, the one true love interest, Rowan Whitethorn, is introduced in book three. In the sprawling timelines of the *Outlander* series, characters also leave and return, like Brianna Fraser, Roger MacKenzie and Ian Murray.

8. Offer payoffs for previous foreshadowing

Throughout the later books in your series, you need to reward your readers with payoffs to previous foreshadowing. Each later book should either build upon existing foreshadowing and breadcrumbs or offer a temporary payoff (at least until the final book). You can also create new foreshadowing and breadcrumbs. Similarly, you should resolve some of the open loops you created in previous books while creating new ones to pull the reader from one sequel to the next.

9. Meaningful deaths

Depending on your genre, your series might need to include a meaningful death or two. Fictional deaths need to be well-planned and well-executed if the reader is going to be emotionally affected.

Think of a death in fiction that gave you a big emotional response. For me, *Game of Thrones* offers numerous examples:

- The beheading of Ned Stark
- The betrayal of Robb and Catelyn Stark at the infamous Red Wedding
- When King Joffrey is killed at his wedding feast
- When Ramsay Bolton gets what's coming to him

Each of these scenes left the audience reeling, either fist-pumping the air with cries of justice served or shocked at the scale of bloodshed and backstabbing. All these instances were powerful because the writers laid the groundwork of characterisation beforehand. Readers and viewers had already emotionally invested in the outcome of the character and story arcs, so when the deaths occurred, the ultimate payoff was immense.

10. Explore more of the world

Depending on your genre and reader expectations, you might like to use your sequel and later books to explore more of the world you've created. This is quite common in the fantasy genre, particularly when the protagonist embarks upon a quest. However, exploration of the world isn't just contained to fantasy. A contemporary romance might see the heroine travel from New York to Paris to find love. A post-apocalyptic novel might show the protagonist travelling across the scorched world. A science fiction series might portray the hero leaving Earth and finding life on Mars. Whatever your genre, series present the opportunity to explore their worlds on a much larger scale.

———

Final thoughts on writing sequels and later books…

As soon as you've got your series starter as polished as possible, hand it off to your beta readers, and while they're reading it and compiling their feedback, start the next manuscript. To be a successful indie author, you always need to be working on the next project and utilising time wisely. As you're working on your sequel and the later books in your series, be sure to use your series bible to keep track of concepts, characters and threads so you don't forget about certain details in the following books.

FIFTEEN

Exit and Expansion Strategies Within a Series

"No one will argue that writing is an easy profession. Getting someone to pay you for your words isn't easy. But there are strategies you can use to simplify the process and transform what you can produce."
—Ryan Holiday, "The 7 Strategies That Helped Me Write 3 Books in 3 Years"

I'VE ALREADY MENTIONED that when I started indie publishing in 2017, I didn't have a long-term strategy. I vaguely knew that I would publish my trilogy, but beyond that I had no game plan, no strategies in place to fuel success and no safety nets in case that success dried up. I've come to learn that authors who are serious about their jobs have all of these things and are prepared to pivot when needed. This is in terms of both business and craft, but in this chapter, we'll be exploring the concept on a craft level, specifically in relation to series.

As we covered earlier, writing series does come with a certain risk factor: what if no one likes it and you've written three books in a planned ten-book series? What if you wrote a duology but the readers want more? What if you can't get that first book off the ground?

We've all had to silence that little voice in our heads that worries about the success of upcoming books. While dealing with this voice of self-doubt as I tried to plan my next series, I realised I needed a strategy in place for two possible outcomes:

1. The series tanked
2. The series hit the big time

For peace of mind, I knew I needed to be able to get off the train if things weren't going well, or alternatively, stay on and head for a new destination if things were taking off. There needed to be a level of flexibility around how many books I released. I also knew this strategising needed to happen in the planning stages, particularly as I intended on writing a longer series this time around. So, here's what I came up with...

Exit strategy

There is a myriad of reasons an author might need to wrap a series up sooner than expected, the main three being poor sales, burnout and extenuating life circumstances. For example: perhaps the first three books in a series did well, but readership has dropped off after that, or perhaps the author has been writing in the same world for years and is tired of it. It may be that the author has become a primary carer of a loved one and just can't commit to writing at the moment. Whatever the reason, a career-minded author is strategic in their approach.

Personally, the last thing I would ever want is to disappoint readers by not finishing a series. In my mind, that's a steadfast way to lose fans and stall the trajectory of a career. However, another way to stall a career is to publish books no one wants to read.

As I pondered the beginning of a new series (in which I would implement a lot of the lessons I've learned that are covered in this book), these big "what if"s bothered me immensely. After releasing just two series, I had seen just how much the experience could vary. It was only after chatting things out with one of my author friends that I realised the only way forward was to have the safety net of an emergency exit strategy. I decided I needed to give myself some sort of "get out of jail free" card that would allow me to gracefully bow out of a series if the need arose.

Which is why, even though I plan to write a nine-book series, I'm going to approach it in series story arcs of three (three sets of trilogies), all the while creating open loops and breadcrumbs that can be used as I extend the series. The idea is that as I publish the first three books in the series, I can monitor how they're doing in terms of sales and critical reception, and assess whether or not to continue with the following books. I can do the same again after the sixth book.

There is more than one way to give yourself an exit strategy. You could contain your initial story arcs to duologies (sets of two). You could structure the books within your series so that each one is its own quest and the series could happily wrap up at the end of any of them. You could limit your subplots and cast, with a mind to grow them upon a certain level of success. This is where the planning stage is so important.

At the time of writing this book, I've spent exactly half of my full-time author career in a global pandemic, which above all else has taught me about not only the unpredictability of this job, but the uncontrollable nature of the world itself. There will always be elements to life we can't master, and so I've found that it's best to be prepared and give yourself a failsafe – just in case.

While it's not foolproof, nor is it an exact science, threading these exit strategies throughout my plans for my upcoming series is certainly better than committing to what would likely be nearly five years of my life with no way out if it was needed. And it has given me peace of mind, or as much peace of mind as an author can have.

I'll point out here that the need for these strategies might depend on the individual author's speed of writing. There are certainly prolific writers in our community who can complete a manuscript within a month or less, so these issues might not be as prominent for them. However, as someone who takes a few months to write a first draft, then a few more for reworks and edits, I felt it was important to have a plan in case problems arose.

This notion of exit strategies is not about failure. It's about giving yourself the flexibility to pivot if things change or go unexpectedly, so you can continue to do what you love.

Expansion strategy

On the other hand, you may experience a whirlwind of success for a series (wouldn't that be nice?), in which case it would be immensely beneficial if you had flexibility to *extend* the series. Again, this is where we see the power of open loops and breadcrumbs. Weave enough of these throughout your multi-book arc to allow yourself to pick up the threads as you start to receive positive feedback in the form of reviews and sales.

No author journey is going to be perfect, and nor should it be – we need to make mistakes if we're going to learn. I don't think I could ever have been as strategic as I am now from the beginning, but if I had been, I definitely would have considered extending my first series in order to ride the wave of its initial success. This was an instance of the "artist" talking over the businesswoman… I believed that because I'd announced that *The Oremere Chronicles* was a trilogy from the beginning, and because the original series arc was complete, there was no other option but to finish where I said I would.

Now, I know better. There was (and still is) plenty of room to continue that series and re-energise the success of the past. It's something that's on the cards for possible future projects.

So, while you need to make sure that each of your books and series contain a complete arc to satisfy readers, I encourage you to leave a few open loops where possible in case you wish to return to the story later down the line. In the event that your series takes off, you want to have left the door ajar, allowing you to return years later if you so wish.

Suggestions on how to expand your series include:

- The introduction of a new threat to the world
- The introduction of a new obstacle for the couple – perhaps one gets their dream job somewhere far away and they now have to try a long-distance relationship?
- A side character becomes the protagonist in a new story arc
- Several years have passed and the original cast face new challenges

SIXTEEN

Writing a Killer Series Ending

"Audiences want closure, if you don't give it to them, if you try to cheat them on the resolution, it doesn't matter how well you pulled off everything else. They will hate you forever. This doesn't mean you have to end your book happily… The point of the denouement isn't happiness or sadness or even wrapping things up neatly. The point is tension relief."
—Rachel Aaron, *2k to 10k: Writing Faster, Writing Better, and Writing More of What You Love*

MASTERING the perfect end to your series is incredibly important. Your readers have stuck with you through multiple books by this point and you want to make sure that they close the final volume satisfied, in awe and, hopefully, with the lingering effects of a "book hangover". Ideally, you also want to impress them enough that they follow you to your next series, or read your backlist, or best of all, seek out your whole body of work. Thus, the ending of your series needs to hit the right notes and be memorable for all the right reasons.

How do you know when to end a series?

During my research for this book, one of the most commonly asked questions I received was "How do you know when to end a series?" For some authors, this decision might come naturally. Perhaps you've planned a certain number of books from the beginning, or perhaps the ending came to you in a lightning bolt of inspiration, or maybe it just *feels* right. In these instances, I suggest trusting your gut. If you're ready to end the series, then it's time to do so before you start to resent it.

However, there are some instances when an author might be unsure if it's time to move on or not. The three most common examples of this are when an author has series fatigue, when real life gets in the way, and when a series isn't doing well sales-wise. In these instances, it might be time to wrap up the current arc (remember when we discussed linked trilogies and duologies as an escape route?) and move onto something new for the time being.

The truth is, no one but the author can really know when it's time to end a series. I encourage you to discuss your options with your beta readers or trusted friends in the industry, but ultimately, like many aspects of this career, the final decision lies with you.

But what if you *are* ready to end your series? How do you ensure you don't disappoint your readers?

Common pitfalls

Endings are tricky. For me, they're the most challenging part of the drafting process, especially when I'm trying to wrap up an entire series. There are a lot of mixed emotions for an author during this time. I generally experience a contrary combination of wanting to hurry up and finish, and then procrastinating because I'm not quite sure how to say goodbye to my characters. During this part of the process, I rely heavily on the feedback of my beta readers. I discuss the ending with them at length. I ask them: are there unanswered questions? What is the lingering feeling that's left behind? Is it satisfying while also not being too neat and tidy?

A bad ending to a series can burn a reader so that they never read your work again. Here are some of the common pitfalls I've seen...

1. Rushed ending

Whether the author has suffered from series fatigue (I'll explain this later) or bad sales, or is just excited to have a complete series under their belt, one of the most common mistakes I've seen is rushed endings. This is where the author wraps everything up too quickly without giving the reader the chance to process their emotions.

I have a tendency to do this in my first draft, but I recognise it easily now by comparing the length of the third act to the first two. If it's significantly shorter, I know that I've rushed parts of it, and that I need to go back and expand upon certain scenes and chapters so the series and character arcs are resolved at a steady pace and the reader experiences lingering emotional resonance.

2. Abrupt ending

An abrupt ending is when the final book ends seemingly out of nowhere. There's no denouement where the reader experiences the completion of the series and character arcs. Similarly to a rushed ending, there's no time for them to process what has happened; the book simply ends. An abrupt ending leaves a reader feeling cheated and stumped as to why, after everything the characters have been through, the author chose to stop there.

I see little reason to end a long-running series like this, though perhaps for some it's a stylistic/artistic choice. However, there's a difference between an ambiguous or open-ended finale and an abrupt or incomplete finish. Don't do the latter to your readers – they likely won't return to your work again.

As the wonderful Rachel Aaron says in *2k to 10k: Writing Faster, Writing Better, and Writing More of What You Love*, "When you come down off something as exciting as a climax, you need time to enjoy your victory."

3. Never-ending ending

We've all read a series end like this, where the author hasn't known when enough is enough. Perhaps they're having trouble saying goodbye to characters that have been with them for years; perhaps they didn't do enough planning at the beginning. Whatever the reason, a never-ending ending is a surefire way to frustrate your readers and undo all the magic you created throughout the series to get to this point. An ending that drags out dilutes the impact of completing series and character arcs. If you're unsure whether your ending drags, check with your beta readers.

4. Deus ex machina

Have you ever read the end of a series where the story arc was resolved by a solution that came out of nowhere? It leaves a bad taste in your mouth and has the potential to ruin a perfectly good series. Also known as "deus ex machina", an ending of convenience is when a dire situation is suddenly solved by an unexpected event or occurrence. It's an easy way to get characters out of harm's way, but it feels cheap to the reader or viewer who has stuck with the series until the final moments. As Robert McKee says in *Story: Substance, Structure, Style, and the Principles of Screenwriting:* "Deus ex machina not only erases all meaning and emotion, it's an insult to the audience."

A working example of this would be if a character in a classic fantasy novel fell off the side of a mountain, only to be saved out of the blue by a spacecraft. This could be problematic for readers, particularly with the unexpected introduction of a completely new (and in this case, implausible) element.

Foreshadowing, breadcrumbs and proper planning help avoid endings that come out of nowhere.

How to achieve a killer series ending

Now that we've covered the common pitfalls to avoid, let's explore what actually makes a great end to a series...

1. Know your genre's conventions

Have I hit you over the head with this enough yet? Genre conventions inform so much of what we write. So when you're considering the end to your series, it should be *the very first thing* you consider. Is there a particular expectation that needs to be fulfilled?

For example, readers of the romance genre expect a happily ever after (HEA) ending, no exceptions. Ask anyone in the romance genre and they'll agree: if there's no HEA, it's not a romance, which means very unsatisfied readers at the end of a series. Readers of fantasy might expect an epic battle. Readers of crime thrillers might expect the murder to be solved and justice to be served.

Return to the research you did earlier. Recall the series you read in your own genre. How did these end? Unresolved? Happy? Sad? Hopeful? Identify what's common and popular in your genre and try to adhere to that convention.

2. Close open loops; resolve foreshadowing; complete the series arc and subplots

If you've done your job right, throughout your series you've threaded open loops and foreshadowing, you've created story and character arcs that span multiple books, and you've woven intricate subplots from book one onwards. The end of the last book in your series is where all of these come together. You need to close those loops, resolve that foreshadowing with an epic payoff and complete the arcs you've introduced over the course of your series.

Now, I'm not saying that everything needs to be tied up in a neat and tidy bow. But you do need to address questions you've asked, and give your readers final moments of character resolution. Whatever your series has been building up to needs to occur and you need to give the reader time to process the finale. The end should be all about rewarding the reader for sticking with you and your characters through all the conflict, obstacles and everything in between.

Is there a character readers will want to see one last time? Give them that. Have they been holding on to hope for a reunion of sorts? Make it happen. You want your readers to finish the final chapter and not know what to do with themselves now your series is over. In order to achieve this, there needs to be satisfaction for the reader.

· · ·

3. Leave some things unsaid; leave room for interpretation

Despite me harping on about closing loops and completing your story arcs, don't fall into the trap of jamming everything into the last chapter or having everything wrap up too neatly. The best series endings leave some things up to the reader to interpret, giving them room to imagine a life for your characters beyond the final page.

For example, in *A Conjuring of Light*, the third instalment of V.E. Schwab's *Shades of Magic* trilogy, the final passages show us Lila and Kell, the protagonists, boarding a ship. Kell describes Lila as "still a mystery", implying there is much more to learn about her as they embark on a new journey together. The series closer ends as this new adventure begins, allowing the reader a moment to breathe and reflect upon all that has happened.

Leaving a few things unsaid allows your fans the space to process the magnitude of the events in your series and the emotions they had to ride out.

4. Leave the door ajar, in case you want to return later

As we explored in the chapter on exit and expansion strategies, there may come a time where you wish to return to your series. Perhaps it takes off sales-wise a few years later; perhaps you get a groundbreaking idea for how to explore a totally different element of the world... The possibilities are endless, so you don't want to close the door permanently, no matter how complete you think the series is at the time. Perhaps there's an element of ambiguity to your ending. Perhaps another adventure awaits in the wings. Perhaps there's a secondary character who has become more prominent in the later books. It might even be as vague as there simply being more of the world to explore.

Interestingly, since the publication of the series finale of the *Shades of Magic* trilogy referenced above, V.E. Schwab has announced the extension of this series with a new trilogy, *Threads of Power*. She left the door ajar in the final passages of the last book, and this has enabled her to continue what was an incredibly successful series.

However you choose to leave the door ajar is up to you, but I recommend that you allow your future self that option, should you need or want it.

5. Make it emotive

Your characters and your readers have likely gone through hell by this point, and your series ending should acknowledge that. The final scenes should be thought-provoking and emotional and should highlight the underlying themes of your whole series. You want this series to stay with your readers long after they finish reading it; you want to be responsible for leaving them nursing a book hangover. You can do this by ramping up the emotional resonance of your final chapters and resolving your character arcs. I would also suggest offering a glimmer of hope, even if it's a sad ending. After everything the characters (and readers) have been through, a glimmer of hope on the horizon is much needed.

A popular example of this is the finale of the TV series *Breaking Bad*, "Felina", where we see Walter White finally do right by his sidekick, Jesse. Walter is shot while helping Jesse escape and is left to bleed out as he reflects on all he has done over the course of five gripping seasons. We are offered a ray of hope with the image of Jesse driving off, free at last, crying with relief and joy.

Another emotional TV series ending is the finale of *Friends*. A decade in the making, the final episode saw audiences fight tears as Ross and Rachel finally got together, Monica and Chandler welcomed twins into the world, and the cast (and viewers) said goodbye to the apartment that had been the show's home for so long.

6. Give a nod to the series beginning/mirror image

A brief nod to the beginning of your series at the end can highlight just how far your characters have come and just how much they've been through. There's a sense of nostalgia in an ending like this – a sense that the readers and characters have come full circle and are able to reflect upon how much they've grown. Often authors end their series in the same setting in which it began, but with the characters having undergone a transformation.

Take *The Lord of the Rings* as an example: *The Fellowship of the Ring* starts with Frodo living his normal life in the Shire, and the finale, *The Return of the King*, sees him return to his homeland a hero, having faced numerous deadly challenges and destroyed the Ring of Power. He is not the same hobbit who left the Shire, nor is his companion, Sam.

The TV show *The Vampire Diaries* does this as well, by repeating the line "Hello, brother" from episode one in the final episode of the last season, highlighting just how much the Salvatore brothers have changed and grown over the course of the series. Rivals at the beginning, they become true brothers by the end.

Friends also does this well in the series finale, with the cast going for coffee at the coffee house where the whole show started.

7. Epilogues

An epilogue offers the author the opportunity to jump forward in time to show the reader the aftermath of the events in the series. It's often a narration-style summary of how everything worked out. If the author has used a prologue, an epilogue can be a natural endpoint to a series. This device is most commonly used in fantasy and sci-fi, but has become increasingly popular in romance too.

In *Harry Potter and the Deathly Hallows*, J.K. Rowling uses an epilogue (as well as the mirror image ending) to wrap up her seven-book series. Nineteen years later, we see Harry, Ginny, Ron and Hermione at King's Cross station, farewelling their children, who are off to Hogwarts. We see that everything has worked out for them after the battle against Voldemort and that the future is bright.

In the final book of my own series, *The Oremere Chronicles*, the epilogue takes place three months after the final battle, where the protagonist, Bleak, at last returns to her true homeland and takes her rightful place as one of the Oremian heirs.

In romance series, the epilogue often involves a wedding or the couple having their first child together.

This is another instance where I encourage you to return to your genre expectations. Are epilogues commonly used? If not, you may want to consider ending your series another way.

Section IV: Long-Term Strategies for Writing Series

"An old maxim says that a professional writer is an amateur who didn't quit."
—Richard Bach, *A Gift of Wings*

SEVENTEEN

Write Longer Series

"A long series can be the difference between writing being a dream and writing being a career."
—Zoe York, *Romance Your Plan: Taking Genre Fiction Marketing to the Next Level*

SOMETHING THAT HAS BECOME apparent to me in recent years is the benefits of writing longer-running series (series that span five or more books). If I could go back in time, I would definitely have considered extending *The Oremere Chronicles*. It is a series that has served me well for years, and now, with more experience under my belt, I know it would have been incredibly advantageous for the series to be five books or more, rather than the standard trilogy. But why?

Why write longer series?

1. Take advantage of the momentum

It takes time for a series to build momentum, both in readership and sales. There are various reasons for this: some readers wait until there are a few books already out before purchasing, others wait until there's more social proof of quality (reviews), and some series just take a while to find their niche audience. Whatever the reason, it's safe to say that most series don't take off overnight – it takes time for sales (and page reads, if you're in Kindle Unlimited) to trickle in.

I found that just as both *The Oremere Chronicles* and *Curse of the Cyren Queen* were really finding their audiences, they ended. I had put all this work into finding a readership for both series, only to end them as things began to kick off. Writing a longer series allows you to take advantage of all the hard work you've put in and the momentum that starts to build with each new release.

2. Revive book one with subsequent launches

Each launch of a new book in a series is the opportunity to relaunch book one and hook new readers into your series sales funnel. A longer series provides you with this opportunity regularly. A reader might see the announcement of book five in the series and love the cover or the blurb, prompting them to find the first book and invest in the series arc from the beginning. Ongoing launches of subsequent books always breathe new life into the series, and authors often experience a surge in sales not only of the newly released title, but of book one as well.

3. Double down on the benefits of writing series

Earlier in this book we explored all the benefits of writing series in general – from the flexibility with promotions, to the opportunity to explore your world on a grander scale, to the ease of utilising your existing groundwork. All the same benefits apply again to writing longer series.

. . .

4. Advertising is even more profitable

As Chris Fox says in his book *Six Figure Author: Using Data to Sell Books*, "The longer my series, the more acceptable a loss on advertising for book one is." We talked earlier about creating loss leaders, which are a popular way for authors to cast the net as wide as possible and eliminate the price barrier to entry for new readers. Writing a longer series increases the likelihood of a higher return on investment in that loss leader. For example, if a reader got the first book for free, the author loses a sale that could have been worth $4.99; however, if that reader then goes on to read six more books at full price, the return on that initial loss is well worth it.

Writing longer series follows the mentality that it's easier to sell 10 books to one person than it is to sell one book to 10 people.

5. The advantages of Kindle Unlimited

While this benefit won't be applicable to everyone, it's certainly worth a mention. For those who don't know, Kindle Unlimited (KU) is a reader subscription service into which authors can enrol their books, making them exclusive to Amazon. This service is designed with a particular type of reader in mind: "whale readers". A whale reader is someone who reads at a much faster rate than normal – they usually get through multiple titles per week and have a tendency to commit to series with lots of books in them. The more books you have in a series in KU, the more lucrative your publishing will be. It's far easier to get a reader to continue a series they're already invested in than to bring them across to start something brand-new.

Examples of longer series

- *The Black Dagger Brotherhood* by J.R. Ward (20 books)
- The *Bridgertons* series by Julia Quinn (eight books)
- *The Wheel of Time* by Robert Jordan and Brandon Sanderson (14 books)
- The *Alex Cross* series by James Patterson (29 books)
- The *Kay Scarpetta* series by Patricia Cornwall (26 books)
- The *Outlander* series by Diana Gabaldon (expected to be 10 books)
- The *In Death* series by J.D. Robb (54 books)

All of these traditionally published authors have enjoyed immense long-term success over the course of their careers, but what about our fellow indies? Which of our colleagues have implemented this strategy to their advantage? Here are a few examples...

- *The Orion War* by M.D. Cooper (13 books)
- The *ARKANE* series by J.F. Penn (12 books)
- *Judge, Jury, & Executioner* by Craig Martelle and Michael Anderle (13 books)
- *Zodiac Academy* by Caroline Peckham and Susanne Valenti (eight books)
- The *DCI Ryan Mystery* series by L.J. Ross (18 books)
- The *Cerberus* series by Andy Peloquin (eight books)
- *The Echoes Saga* by Philip C. Quaintrell (nine books)

Tips for writing longer series

- In your planning stage, choose an intriguing central

conflict that has enough substance to sustain multiple books

- Remember expectations for your chosen genre – in fantasy, longer series aren't surprising, but you may find in romance and other genres that readers are hesitant; combat this by writing interconnected standalones
- Make sure you're writing what you love – this will sustain you if things get tough

To summarise: use breadcrumbs, open loops and soft cliffhangers to drive your readers from one volume to the next. Ensure that each book within the series has its own satisfying arc, while asking a new question to keep the reader intrigued. Craft compelling characters so the reader emotionally invests in their arcs and is desperate to know how it all works out for them. Raise the stakes with each book and test your characters to breaking point.

EIGHTEEN

Your Second Series and Beyond

"I can promise you that if you keep building on what you have done in the past, rather than starting over, you will see momentum. Stick to your plan. Stick to what gets you excited, and keep building. Write Series 2.0. And then, Series 3.0. Keep writing."
—Zoe York, *Romance Your Brand: Building a Marketable Genre Fiction Series*

IF YOU'RE anything like me, you might have a new idea waiting in the wings for when you finish your current work in progress. Maybe you like to work on several projects at once, or perhaps you like to start with a blank page each time. Whatever your process, before you launch yourself into your next series, I ask you to pause and consider a concept that author Zoe York discusses in her book *Romance Your Brand*, and that's "Series 2.0". In a nutshell, the concept involves studying your first series and improving upon it. York encourages authors to think about what they shied away from in that first series because of their inexperience, or what they had originally deemed too commercial but are now keen on to make more sales, and to explore these elements in more depth.

This is a brief chapter in her book, but it resonated with me deeply. While I had grown as a writer from my first series to my second and implemented a lot of the craft, production and publishing lessons I'd learned along the way, something didn't translate between the two works. While both my series are YA fantasy and take place in the same wider world, in hindsight, I suspect my *Curse of the Cyren Queen* series veered a little too far from my original concept in *The Oremere Chronicles*.

The *Cyren Queen* series is centred around mythical siren-like creatures rather than human magic wielders. It's just a few steps too far removed from what my fans had come to love about *Oremere*. Focusing on these creatures added a learning curve for readers to overcome. It wasn't until I read *Romance Your Brand* (halfway through writing *Curse of the Cyren Queen*) that I was able to put my finger on this point of difference and take an educated guess as to why the performance of the two series had varied.

Looking back, I was so buzzed by the success of *The Oremere Chronicles* that I wanted to launch straight into writing the new series. I had the idea, I had numerous lessons under my belt and I wanted to keep up the sales momentum. What I should have done was hit pause and examine what people were loving about that first series. As York says: "Look at your series, and tweak it. Think … what would the [X number of] fans who loved Series 1.0 want to see in Series 2.0?"

That's not to say that *Curse of the Cyren Queen* didn't find its readers. It did and continues to do so today, but I suspect that I isolated some of my existing readers by veering a little too far off the path I had laid before. So, what do I recommend?

I want to build upon the advice Zoe York outlined in *Romance Your Brand*. Your first series is out in the world. It has a handful of fans, and you're proud of it. However, no matter how much preparation and outlining you did for it, it was still your *first* series. There was a huge learning curve; mistakes were made... Before you start your next series, identify those lessons you learned and those mistakes you made, and make note of how you can avoid them the second time around. Ask yourself:

- What are the common complaints in my reviews? What can I improve upon?
- What did my readers love? How can I give them more of this?
- How was the length of my series received? Could it have been longer?
- What are the titles my book is being compared to? (Read those titles and their reviews. Take notes)

These questions and answers can be added to your initial research and planning for your new series. The point is that you're always striving to improve your craft and the experience for your readers.

I also found that the more books I had out, the less time I had for actual writing. My time was taken up by responding to emails (usually from readers asking when the next instalment was due out); running reviewer outreach campaigns; managing content marketing, advertising, social media... All of which served to maintain the status of the current books, but none of which saw to the growth of my series and overall catalogue.

Once you publish your series starter, the clock starts ticking and suddenly you're part of a much bigger production merry-go-round. It's incredibly easy to lose your writing time to the various other tasks a career author has to do. So, as you're working your way through your first series, you should also be learning about *how* you work. When it's time to start your second, ask yourself:

- Did I get stuck at a particular point during writing? How can I combat this?
- Is there any way I can improve my workspace?
- Is there any way I can improve my overall processes to optimise production?
- Do I need different beta readers?
- Did production halt at any point? If so, why? How can this be avoided next time?

To be a career author is to be constantly learning – about writing, about the industry, about yourself. You need to be producing books on a regular basis. As artistic as writing a book is, publishing is a business, and you need to be able to run yours effectively and efficiently.

NINETEEN

The Power of the Reader Magnet

"They're an irresistible force that draw readers in − the promise of getting great value content and building a valuable connection. That's what it's all about, after all − making meaningful connections with your audience and creating a direct line to your readers..."
—Nick Stephenson, *Reader Magnets: Build Your Author Platform and Sell more Books on Kindle (2022 Edition)*

SOME OF YOU probably won't be shocked to learn that the *writing* aspect of writing a series isn't simply contained to the books within that series. If you want long-term success in this industry, I believe there's another element you have to master: the reader magnet.

In my experience, reader magnets play a crucial role in the success of a series and have the power to contribute to an author's entire career. I'd know − I've used them to great effect myself. But first, what is a reader magnet?

In indie publishing, a reader magnet is something that you give to your potential readers for free in exchange for their email address. Sometimes they're also referred to as lead magnets (or "cookies" thanks to Tammi L. Labrecque and her book *Newsletter Ninja*).

A reader magnet can be just about anything – a novella, a short story, a character profile, a character interview, fictional police files, a fantasy map, character art. The purpose of this content is twofold: to start building a warm audience by offering potential readers a free trial or "taste" of your work in exchange for signing up to your mailing list *and* to reward existing readers of a series who are waiting for the next book.

When I started out, I had done enough research to know I needed a reader magnet before I published. I wrote a short story, "Break", which served as a prequel to my first book, *Heart of Mist*. It was roughly 4,000 words and took place a few years before the events of the main series. I didn't have an overly big following on social media, nor was I aware of the list-building tools that are widely available now. Regardless of this, the story was incredibly effective in getting people onto my mailing list before I'd even launched book one. So much so that I wrote another, and another.

Before *Heart of Mist* released in August 2017, I had promoted these exclusive short stories to my social media pages and built a modestly sized but super-engaged subscriber list. The majority of people on this list were keen to find out about the protagonist, Bleak, whom I'd introduced in these reader magnets.

Ever since, I've been utilising the power of the reader magnet to:

- Feed new readers into the sales funnel of each of my series
- Reward the readers who love the series on a deep level
- Keep readers entertained and interested in between releases

For *The Oremere Chronicles*, I sent my mailing list nine prequel stories in total over the years that the main series was being released: three before *Heart of Mist* launched, three in between books one and two, and three again between books two and three.

Not only was this strategy bringing new readers to my mailing list, but it kept my existing readers engaged and satisfied throughout the year between releases. As a side benefit, it also helped me develop my characters on a much deeper level.

For *Curse of the Cyren Queen*, I released three prequel novellas in the lead up to the release of book one. Having learned the power of the reader magnet the first time around, I took these next prequels far more seriously. I had professional covers designed for them and formatted them for all devices (previously I'd just done plain PDFs and no covers), and I had them all copyedited and proofread. As a not-so-beginner author at this stage, I also had the knowledge to utilise platforms like BookFunnel, where you can feature your reader magnets in group giveaways in order to gain email subscribers and hook new readers into your series.

To me, a good reader magnet is a shorter work (like a short story or, preferably, a novelette or novella) that introduces the reader to the world of your series. It should do the following…

1. Offer a complete experience

As Tammi L. Labrecque suggests in *Newsletter Ninja: How to Become an Author Mailing List Expert*: "Give [readers] a complete experience… Give them an entire story – a short story, novella, or entire novel – so they know you can not only write an intriguing beginning or sample, but that you can actually wrap up a story in a satisfying fashion."

This is mainly in reference to authors who offer the first chapter or chapters of their book for free instead of a short story or novella. Authors who only offer samples miss the opportunity to showcase their complete skillset to their potential readers. As Labrecque says: offer the complete experience, a story that has a beginning, middle and end, to demonstrate that your full-length work will do the same. You need to prove to your readers that you can master structure and pacing as well as character and prose.

My first reader magnet "Break" was a complete short story, though in hindsight, it's certainly not my best work. It did the job, though, and as I progressed in my reader magnet journey, each piece got longer and more well-rounded, offering the reader a story complete with a resolution, as well as a promise for more stories in the future.

2. Bridge the gap between the reader, the first book and subsequent books

A reader magnet can be used as a clever tactic to bridge the gap between the reader and the first book in a series. This is something I've done quite well with my reader magnets over the years, if I do say so myself.

Before *Heart of Mist* was released, I sent my subscribers three prequel stories featuring the main character, a young woman called Bleak. "Break", "The Gift" and "Felder's Bay" introduce us to who Bleak is, as well as showing us one of the main settings and the position of magic in the world (forbidden). The reader is given insight into several pivotal moments in our heroine's life that impact who she becomes in the main series. By the time book one was released, readers were invested in Bleak's story and wanted to know more – thus I bridged the gap between my readers and *Heart of Mist* before the book was even out.

I took this a step further. Back in 2017, I knew I would only be able to publish one book a year, which could be considered a slow pace for an indie. I also knew that I had to keep my audience warm and interested in my story in between publications. So I kept writing prequels. These only took me a few days to write and then I sent them off to my editor. I wrote another one from Bleak's point of view before turning to the rest of my cast. *The Oremere Chronicles* is a multi-POV series, and so I also wrote prequels from other points of view: "Viper's Kiss", "The King's Tournament" and "Willowdale" are all from the perspective of Commander Swinton, while "The Valian Heir", "The Valian Way" and "The Heart of the Forest" are all from warrior queen Henri's point of view.

Each story focuses on a life-changing moment that shapes each protagonist into the character we meet in the main series. For example, in the first story, "Break", we see Bleak use her long-hated mind reading power to save her best friend Bren from a watery grave. It's in this story that her guardian tells her that her magic is "a gift", something she recalls bitterly in the main series but eventually comes to accept.

Bleak's prequel stories continue to show us pivotal moments in her life. In "The Gift", we follow her as she tries to find a cure for her powers from a famous healer, and we are introduced to the legend of magic wielder Casimir and the trickster known as the Tailor – two characters who play vital roles in the later *Oremere* books. And the healer? She plays a role too, and is also referenced in my *Curse of the Cyren Queen* series.

In the story "Felder's Bay", we're introduced to the deadly mist – the overarching threat of the main series – in the flesh for the first time, plus we get a glimpse of Bleak and Bren's relationship evolving into something more than friendship, which is important for their friction in *Heart of Mist*. In "Savage Seas", we meet Maz, one of the series' antagonists, and we experience the tragic death of Bleak's guardian, whom she still mourns in the main series.

As I hope you can see, each prequel offers a kernel of knowledge, shedding light onto important events in the characters' lives that have great meaning in the main series.

In between publishing my full-length books, I released these prequel stories to my email subscribers, free of charge. It was one of the best things I've done. It not only kept my original readers fascinated with the characters' backstories, but drew new readers to my mailing list as more and more free stories became available.

The most popular of my prequel stories were those that explored the big events in a character's past, which were referenced but never fully explained in the full-length novels. For example:

- The death of a loved one
- A failed mission
- The uncovering of an awful truth
- A villain origin story
- The inciting incident of a lifelong dream

For the *Oremere* prequels, I didn't have a set word count or goal for each story – I just wrote each one as it demanded to be written. With *Curse of the Cyren Queen*, I knew I wanted the reader magnets to be closer to novelettes/novellas than short stories, so I planned them in more detail from the outset. However, because of their length (closer to 14,000 words each), they were more expensive and time-consuming to produce, so I only wrote three.

Longer reader magnets will feel like higher-value items to your subscribers, but it's entirely up to you how you choose to approach your own. The length depends on the type of story you're writing, how many you plan to create for each series, and how much you can physically produce in between books.

3. Use reader magnets to link two different series

As I've progressed through my career, I've also learned that a reader magnet can be utilised in an even more strategic way. You can use a reader magnet to bridge the gap between one series and another (provided it's set in the same world), making it more likely that a reader will follow you from one series to the next.

I implemented this technique between *The Oremere Chronicles* and *Curse of the Cyren Queen*. It involved taking a setting and a race of creatures that played a vital role in *War of Mist* (final *Ormere* book) and spotlighting them in my three free prequel novellas, *Cyren Queen Origins* (linked to at the end of the *Oremere* series and "released" to my existing mailing list). These novellas took elements readers were familiar with and built upon them in a way that readied them for what was to come in the new series, essentially leading them by the hand both to my mailing list and into my next story.

Earlier in my career I did this on a much smaller scale with references throughout my previous prequel stories. For example, in the *Oremere* prequel "A Current So Strong", a famous fiddler duo is mentioned: the Eery Brothers. They are due to perform in Bleak's town and the villagers are buzzing. Bleak and Bren dance to their songs later that night – an important milestone for them. The Eery Brothers are then referenced in the main *Oremere Chronicles* series because they're part of that key memory; however, in *Curse of the Cyren Queen*, the Eery Brothers appear again, taking on a much bigger role in the story.

4. Reflect your tone/style for the books that follow

Another benefit of the reader magnet is that it gives readers a taste of what your writing tone/style/voice is like, which is why it's important that your magnets reflect the style (and quality) of your books.

For example, all my reader magnets are in close third person, past tense, as are my books. There would be no point writing in a different style to that of the books I eventually want to sell these readers. They need to know from reading my magnet that they'll enjoy my style of writing *before* they purchase the full-length book.

5. Introduce your work with no barrier to entry

Reader magnets provide authors with the unique opportunity to introduce their readers to their fiction without any barrier to entry besides providing their email address. It's one of the best ways you can pique a reader's interest in your protagonist and their world without asking for money straight away.

By the time *Heart of Mist* launched, I had nearly 1,000 warm leads (keen readers) who were invested in Bleak as a character and wanted to see her story unfold. My reader magnets had turned strangers into readers who were willing to open their wallets for a book by an unknown author. Without the free prequel stories being sent to my mailing list, I'm not sure *Heart of Mist* would have had the same initial reception that it did.

Reader magnet mistakes to avoid

As with any aspect of this career, there are learning curves when writing reader magnets. Here are some of the mistakes I made early on...

- Not knowing how many magnets I was going to write per series and therefore not choosing the most pivotal moments in a character's history to explore
- Not keeping the word counts consistent. My original reader magnets range from 4,000 words to 14,000 words long. The longer ones are always more popular, so now I aim for novella length (10,000+ words) in order to package my reader magnets in a way that displays the most value
- Not making the reader magnet about the main character in the main series. For *Curse of the Cyren Queen*, I wrote a trilogy of prequel novellas, *Cyren Queen Origins*, that focused on Cerys, the mother of the main series' protagonist, and Deelie, the queen of the main series. These have been incredibly popular, but I've noted that some readers are still desperate for Cerys and Deelie's full story, and some expected *Curse of the Cyren Queen* to be about these two characters rather than Cerys' daughter, Roh
- Not planning the stories. The prequels for *The Oremere Chronicles* were written quite haphazardly and without much forethought. That became problematic the deeper into the main series I got and the more prequels I wrote. Some additional planning would have made things easier for me

Tips for powerful reader magnets

- Feature the protagonist that your main books will be about, if you can; pique the reader's curiosity about that character
- Create a timeline for the events in the main series and

the events that precede those books (use your series bible!). This will make it easier to position your prequels in a canon of events for the whole world

- Have your reader magnet professionally edited. While it may seem like an expense that won't see a direct financial return, it will create a polished product that accurately reflects the quality of your full-length work, and the payoff will be eager readers ready to read your main series

- If possible, have covers created for your reader magnets that match your main series. Again, I realise it's an additional expense, but it makes getting readers onto your mailing list so much easier when you have a visual product to advertise. The prequels for *The Oremere Chronicles* had no covers – they were just simple PDFs; for *Cyren Queen Origins*, I had professional covers made, and it made a world of difference

TWENTY

Create a Flagship or Anchor Series

"An anchor series is a well-branded, clearly defined series with five or more books that is positioned to bring in readers and income to your career for years to come."
—Sarra Cannon, "How To Write A Best-Selling Series (And What Is An Anchor Series?)"

OVER THE COURSE of writing and publishing my first two series, I've started to look to the future long term. I know I want to sustain this career for years to come; I want to be able to pay off a mortgage and save for retirement – ideally, I'd even like to be able to send my partner to university to study winemaking (the dream, right?). Through my experiences with releasing a trilogy and a quartet, I've come to learn that publishing longer series would be more beneficial, both financially and creatively. But as I delved deeper into the broader concept of series writing, I discovered something else – something bigger and better: the power of a flagship series.

What is a flagship series?

A "flagship" series is the series that carries an author's career throughout the years. It's the one that continually outsells all the other titles in their catalogue. According to Chris Fox, who coined the term at the Sell More Books Show Summit, a flagship series should tally over one million words in total. There is no set number of books it should span, as this depends on the length of your books and your genre.

Author Sarra Cannon (who I've quoted above) refers to this concept as an "anchor" series, but the idea is much the same: a longer series that acts as an author's primary earner.

Another defining aspect of a flagship series is that it offers a big world that attracts passionate readers who not only purchase every title in the series, but also help publicise the work via social media, stellar reviews and word of mouth. In his talk at the Sell More Books Show Summit, Chris Fox discussed the high profit margins of flagship series when it comes to advertising. Because of the high read-through rates of flagship series, authors are more likely to make ads profitable on any platform, enabling them to sell these books long after the initial release – ideally for the rest of their lives. If the series is really successful, there's even a chance the author won't have to work again.

Another advantage we've already touched on when it comes to larger series is the ease of expansion. It's much easier for an author to deepen the sales funnel and continue the momentum of an existing series. But what are some examples?

Examples of flagship series

The following are examples of published flagship series by indie and traditional authors:

- *The Dresden Files* by Jim Butcher
- The *John Milton* series by Mark Dawson
- *A Song of Ice and Fire* by George R.R. Martin
- *The Kurtherian Gambit* by Michael Anderle
- *Death Before Dragons* by Lindsay Buroker
- The *Harry Potter* series by J.K. Rowling
- *The Mortal Instruments* by Cassandra Clare
- *Vampire Academy* by Richelle Mead

When to start your flagship series

If you're reading this book as you're working on your first series or you're still at the planning stage, don't panic. I know we indies experience an inner pressure to do *all the things* straight away, but I want you to pause for a moment. A flagship series is not something you need to rush into or attempt as the first work of your career. It's a long-game strategy – one that usually works best after an author already has a published series or two under their belt.

There is such a giant learning curve when it comes to writing and publishing, and to a newer author, attempting a flagship series can seem incredibly daunting. I started out with shorter series, which seemed far less intimidating in terms of not only length, but the associated risks of publishing. Shorter series are a fantastic way to master the basics of series writing and learn your own processes. No matter how experienced an author is, they tend to learn something new about craft, marketing and themselves with each book they write. These lessons are invaluable, particularly if you learn them *before* you try to write a flagship series. You want to be able to gather as much knowledge as you can through your earlier works to inform how you approach your flagship series later. This strategy will give you the best chance at long-term success.

Double your pre-production efforts

A flagship series requires even more time and effort in the pre-production stage than a regular series. It's a more intensive process because your flagship series needs to be your best work yet. You need to have a clear, intentional approach to producing and releasing it.

Use the knowledge you already have not only from your publishing experience, but from your interaction with the readers of your previous works. Hone in on what they loved about your first books and develop it further to weave throughout the new flagship series. Ask yourself how you're going to grow. A flagship series is all about taking your career to the next level.

The core elements of a flagship series

According to Chris Fox, the core elements of a flagship series are a strong narrative drive, open loops and a cast of well-rounded characters. We've already discussed these elements in earlier chapters, but let's take a moment to review them with the length and breadth of a flagship series in mind...

A strong narrative drive

In order to sustain a series for a million words (or thereabouts), you need to have an incredibly strong narrative drive. As the series progresses, the story must increase in complexity and draw the reader in for the long haul. In the case of a flagship series, your narrative spanning multiple books shouldn't just be a series of events, but rather a richly complex story that keeps readers engaged for many books.

Don't make the mistake of overcomplicating the first book in your series or jam-packing it with too many different events or subplots. The complexity can grow as the series expands over time. The last thing you want is to bog your reader down from that first book and kill their desire to read on.

Open loops

We covered open loops in detail earlier, so go back if you need a refresher. However, in flagship series more than any other form, creating numerous open loops is crucial, as these pose questions that need to be answered as the series progresses, spurring the reader on from one book to the next.

A cast of well-rounded characters

If you're going to write over a million words in one series, you need to provide yourself with a quality ensemble cast to sustain you across this endeavour. I'm not just talking about a well-developed protagonist, but a broader cast of secondary characters who all have their own roles, motivations and goals that they're working towards. Each of your characters should have their own drive, as over the course of the series, you may find they need to fill larger roles or act as a catalyst for a big plot twist.

This also allows for conflict (another driving force of a narrative) to brew between all your characters, not just the hero and the antagonist. Shifting alliances between various players creates intrigue that will have readers racing through the story.

A strong brand

While this book is largely focused on the writing side of creating a series, the topic of branding has to be mentioned here. There's no point in writing and publishing a series of such epic proportions if you're not going to brand it well. From the outset, judging by the covers, titles and book descriptions, a reader should be able to tell at a glance that these books all belong together.

Authors usually utilise several of the following to create a uniform brand:

- The same typography/fonts
- Consistent titling conventions (more on this in the FAQs section)
- Consistent colour palette (that matches your genre)
- The same graphics across multiple platforms and social media
- The same tone/style in all book descriptions and advertising/website copy

Final thoughts on flagship series

When it comes to strategising for a successful long-term career as an indie author, having a flagship series is the way to go. From my research and what I see on a regular basis in our industry, most six- and seven-figure authors have a series that's the primary earner in their catalogue, and this is absolutely what I intend to do in the next stages of my own career.

Once an author has a successful flagship series, they can go on to create a flagship *world*, which leads us nicely into our next section...

Section V: Leveraging Literary Universes, Same-World and Second-Generation Series

"What can you create today that will build your body of work?"
— Joanna Penn, *The Successful Author Mindset: A Handbook for Surviving the Writer's Journey*

TWENTY-ONE

What are Literary Universes, Same-World and Second-Gen Series?

"All of my Cosmere books share a single creation myth, a single cosmology, that gives underlying theorem of magic for all these connected worlds."
—Brandon Sanderson, "What is the Cosmere?"

NO MATTER where you're at in your career, I want you to stop for a moment and step back to consider the bigger picture. You might have a series or two under your belt already; perhaps you're still working on your first… Or perhaps you haven't even put pen to paper yet. But a career author is always thinking: *What comes next?*

If there's one thing Tolkien, J.K. Rowling and Stan Lee taught me, it's the power of the literary universe, which can become an author's personal empire if they play their cards right.

Literary universes, flagship worlds and same-world series

To me, a literary universe and a "same-world" series are one and the same: a collection of work spanning multiple series that are set in the same world. That's it. A flagship world is pretty much the same, with the added detail of it being the most prominent creation in an author's body of work.

There are so many well-known examples of this literary technique:

- *Harry Potter*, *The Cursed Child* and *Fantastic Beasts* by J.K. Rowling
- *The Vampire Diaries* and *The Originals* (TV shows)
- *The Hobbit* and *The Lord of the Rings* by J.R.R. Tolkien (or the films directed by Peter Jackson)
- Any of the Marvel/*Avengers* IP created by Stan Lee, Jack Kirby and Steve Ditko
- *The Farseer Trilogy*, *The Liveship Traders*, *The Tawny Man*, *The Rain Wild Chronicles* and *Fitz and the Fool*, which are all part of *The Realm of the Elderlings* by Robin Hobb
- *The Stormlight Archive*, *The Mistborn Trilogy*, *Mistborn: Wax and Wayne* and the *White Sand* graphic novels, which are all part of Brandon Sanderson's Cosmere universe

Let's look at a few of those in more detail.

Whether via the *Harry Potter* books, films or both, most of us are familiar with the boy wizard who discovers a secret world of magic within his ordinary one: a world where there are schools for magic, fantastical creatures, wizards and witches with wands, and so forth. Now look at *Fantastic Beasts and Where to Find Them* – the book version is a textbook that is referenced throughout the main series, while the film version is set in the same world as *Harry Potter*. It adheres to the same rules of magic and the same societal structure, and even features some of the same characters. Finally, the play, *Harry Potter and the Cursed Child*, is set 19 years after the events in the last Harry Potter book. It features an adult

Harry Potter, now working at the Ministry of Magic, and his youngest son, Albus Severus Potter, who is about to start his first year at Hogwarts School of Witchcraft and Wizardry. (This is also a fantastic example of "second generation" stories, wherein the protagonist featured is the child or relative of one of the main characters in the previous series – more on that shortly.)

Each of these stories built upon the world J.K. Rowling created and tapped into an existing fandom, launching to an already keen audience as well as breathing new life back into the original series. Most fans were familiar with the world and eager to return to it, in one form or another.

How about the Marvel films? Over the first New Zealand lockdown of 2020, my partner and I decided to watch all the Marvel superhero films in chronological order. It's incredibly rewarding to see certain characters crop up in other heroes' storylines and to notice the references to previous events in the canon – perhaps it's because you start to feel like part of an "inner circle". While you can watch most of these films on their own, you enjoy them more and more when you have the context of the other films. I'd seen a handful of Marvel films over the years, enjoying the individual series like *Iron Man* and *Captain America* on their own merit, but together… I was hooked. And by the time I got to *Endgame*, I was 100% invested and consequently in pieces when it was over.

As for indie author examples, how about M.D. Cooper's *Aeon 14 Universe*? This comprises several series set in particular "ages" within the broader literary world, such as the Age of the Sentience Wars, the Second Age of Colonization and the Age of Terra, to name a few.

And it's not just fantasy and sci-fi that utilise this approach. Plenty of successful indie romance authors use the same town setting for multiple series, or take a secondary character from a happily-ever-after story and give them their own time in the spotlight. A great example in the romance genre is New Zealand author Anne Malcom. At the time of writing, she has three separate series in her *Sons of Templar* universe: *Sons of Templar MC*, *Unquiet Mind* and *Greenstone Security*, all featuring character and location crossovers.

Second-generation series

A second-generation series technically falls under the same umbrella as same-world series, but I think it deserves its own mention. It's become an increasingly popular method that romance authors in particular use to expand their catalogue into new stories, while keeping their original fanbase.

A second-generation series is pretty much what it sounds like. It takes the next generation from the original cast of characters and makes the children (usually grown up) the protagonists of the new series. The new series features the characters the audience knows and loves from the original books as secondary characters, so there's still that element of familiarity, while shifting focus to the younger generation with a whole new host of problems.

A great example of this is the 2021 *Gossip Girl* reboot, which takes place nearly a decade after the original series. While the show features a brand-new ensemble cast, the previous characters still exist in this world and can be referenced freely, not to mention potentially reappear.

My experience so far

Being exposed to these types of same-world series early on must have started the cogs turning in my mind as I started down this career path. I found that as I wrote my fantasy series, I left certain things open-ended or details unexplained, though at the time, I probably couldn't have told you why. It's become more obvious to me now.

In my own work, *The Oremere Chronicles* and *Curse of the Cyren Queen* are set in the same literary universe. There are subtle references (breadcrumbs) to shared locations, magical creatures and types of magic that span both series. For example, a beast we get to know in the second book of *The Oremere Chronicles* – a wild cat I dubbed a "teerah panther" – also shows up in the second and third books of *Curse of the Cyren Queen,* with specific references to where it might have come from (a pivotal plot point in the Oremere books). In the fourth *Cyren Queen* book, the main group of companions travel to a place called Lamaka's Basin, which is referenced heavily in the third and final book of my debut series – in fact, the final scene of the epilogue takes place there. While it may not sound like much, these instances start to add up, creating a broader universe outside of the single book or series a reader is devouring at the time and sparking curiosity about what else is out there in the world the author has created.

These are all small moving parts in a much larger universe-building strategy, and the further into my books I get, the more it will become apparent to the reader. It's my intention to set the next series I write in that same world as well, and eventually have a series that brings them all together. Each book and series works towards expanding my readership, increasing my income and making the launches of any future titles all the more impactful. That, my friends, is the endgame.

TWENTY-TWO

Why Use the Same World?

"Don't look at your work as a series of individual pieces that either 'go big' or flop. Instead, look at it as a body of work. Your magnum opus doesn't have to be a single creation. It can be many creations that when all pieced together say something unique that the world has never before heard."
—Jeff Goins, "Stop Trying to Be Famous and Build a Body of Work Instead"

AS AN AUTHOR WRITING a series (eventually a longer series and/or a flagship series, hopefully), you're likely to build up a loyal following over the course of publishing your books: fans who get invested in the world you've built, in the characters you've created – which is likely one of the reasons you opted for a series in the first place. But it doesn't have to end there, and if you're strategic, it won't. Using the same world for your next series has numerous benefits...

1. It creates multiple entry points to your body of work

Throughout your career, depending on the lengths of the series you write, it can get harder and harder to get new readers to pick up an older series starter. People have a tendency to veer towards the fresh and new. Therefore it makes sense, as part of a broader strategy, to offer multiple starting points to your body of work. We'll talk more about creating a body of work shortly, but essentially, this creates continual chances to find new readers and introduce them to your backlist titles.

2. You're not relying on your weakest book

No matter how hard we try, or how much we invest in editing, often our first book is our weakest. It's where we were still figuring out our world, our characters... Still figuring out ourselves, too! Therefore, one of the benefits of writing a same-world series is that it means you don't have to rely on that single book to draw in your readers to all your work. Someone who was introduced to your work at your tenth published book, upon discovering you have more series set in the same universe, might be inclined to go back to your first-ever book and read through your whole catalogue.

3. It adds to your existing worldbuilding

Particularly in the fantasy and sci-fi genres (though I'd argue for all), writing multiple series set in a common world adds to your original worldbuilding, making it much richer and more dynamic. This, in turn, rewards your loyal readers. Finding those breadcrumbs and clues in previous series they've read makes them all the more keen to venture into new series in the same world to see how it's all drawn together.

4. It makes writing easier

One thing I have loved about writing in the same literary universe is that there is an existing foundation of "rules" when it comes to magic and physical settings. I've been able to build upon that, of course, but it certainly hasn't been as strenuous as starting from scratch and having to come up with a brand-new world. To me, it makes complete sense to utilise the work you've already done – it's equally beneficial to you and the reader.

5. It utilises your flagship series

Not all series are equal in their success. Over the course of their careers, most authors eventually find they have a flagship series – the one that "takes off" and finds a bigger audience than the rest of their books. Writing in the same world across multiple series allows you to take advantage of your flagship series' readership and funnel them towards your other books.

6. It builds your backlist faster

This benefit overlaps with a few of the others, but it's important enough to stand on its own as well. When you're writing in the same world, because of the nature of worldbuilding and planning, you can become a faster writer the more you write in that universe, therefore enabling you to grow your backlist at a much faster rate. And folks, backlist is king. The more titles you have in your backlist, the more opportunities readers have to discover your work, not to mention the more books you have to offer those keen readers (and the more money in your pocket).

TWENTY-THREE

How to Lead Your Readers from Series to Series in Your Literary Universe

"Making the world feel absolutely real to the reader... that's part of the magic of storytelling.. When they're within that fictional world that you have created they long for it to be real and to wish they never had to leave."
—Kate Forsyth, "So You Want to be a Writer", Episode 21

ONE OF MY main concerns when I first started down the "literary universe" path was finding a way to inform my readers that all my series were set in the same world. As I mentioned earlier, on Amazon we have a series page, but this doesn't account for literary universes. There's no way (yet) to tell your audience via retailers that multiple series in your body of work are connected (besides whatever is generated in your "Also Boughts"), so it's up to the author to relay this information to their readership. But how?

Let me share some methods with you now.

Clues within the books

There are a handful of techniques you can use between the covers of your books to ready the reader for a new series set in that same world. The following methods can be as subtle or as overt as you like. When I moved from one series to the next in the same world, I was quite understated with these clues at the beginning. I didn't want to alienate people who hadn't read the first series and discovered me through the second, but I also wanted to reward the readers who had been with me from the start by using breadcrumbs they'd recognise. It's a delicate balance, but one you'll learn how to manage the more books and series you write.

Here are some of the clues I used within my books to connect series in the same universe…

Maps

One of my more brilliant ideas was during the creation of my books' maps. When I wrote *Oremere*, I had no idea what I'd do next – I was simply focused on writing the next book in the current series. However, one thing I knew was that I wanted to keep it as open as possible, so when my map designer asked what I should title the map, I answered "The Upper Realm"… Pretty vague, right? And I'm glad it was, because it gave me flexibility when it came to naming the map for *Curse of the Cyren Queen*… Yep, I went with "Lower Realms". (What do you think will come next? I'm thinking of something like "Mid Realm"… You get the idea.) In any case, you can actually match the map from the *Oremere* books up with the one from the *Curse of the Cyren Queen*.

It's not rocket science by any means, but it has created ample room for me to set multiple series in the same literary universe without much complication. Plus, it means those readers who stick with me throughout my career get a real thrill whenever they notice clues like these.

Cameos

A cameo role is a brief appearance of a well-known actor in a TV show or film. However, many authors utilise this technique in their books as well.

Often in multiple series set in the same literary universe, we'll see familiar characters from previous series featuring as secondary characters or making cameo appearances in a different series further into an author's body of work. Stephen King does this with his character Randall Flagg (also known as the Man in Black), who is the main antagonist in the King multiverse. Flagg is featured in the standalone novels *The Stand* and *The Eyes of the Dragon* as well as several volumes in *The Dark Tower* series.

Authors have the luxury of extending this technique to popular settings, creatures and even memorable phrases, too. Often in fiction, a setting can feel like a character to readers, so referencing or visiting favourite locations across the span of your series can also be a great way to bridge the gap between the various storylines.

I've used this technique myself to pique readers' interest in a new series set in the same world. I've included cameos of key players who will feature in the upcoming book. For example, in *War of Mist* (the final book in *The Oremere Chronicles*), we're introduced to a race of creatures called lisloiks (also known as cyrens); towards the end of the book, we meet their ruler, Queen Delja, who plays a major role in *Curse of the Cyren Queen*... And in my most recent book, *To Wield a Crown* (the final book in *Curse of the Cyren Queen*), we meet a stranger who saves our protagonist's life. This stranger – you guessed it – turns out to be the protagonist of the series that comes next, which I also plan to be my flagship series.

As you can imagine, all of these techniques take some planning and finessing, but the general idea is this: pique your reader's curiosity so they're left wondering about that open loop. After all, they're familiar with the world, and if they've seen a glimpse of a character they might get to know better, they're more likely to be tempted to give your next series starter a shot.

A reading list and/or an author's note

Once you've got a few books/series under your belt, including a reading list in the back matter can be a great way to draw readers' attention to the rest of your work. You can provide a preferred reading order and an explanation if you like. You also have the option to include an author's note, which can shed some behind-the-scenes light on the canon of the series and how it all fits together. Reading lists and author's notes don't require much effort and can serve as a checklist for a reader who has newly discovered your work.

You also don't have to restrict this list to just the book itself. If it's important, you can repurpose it to feature in descriptions for retailers, on your website and even on your social media.

Clues outside the books

While I'm not going to delve too deeply into publishing and marketing strategies (that's another book entirely), I do want to touch on a handful of options you can keep in mind as you build your backlist and collection of series.

Prequel and spin-off series

These types of series can also have their place amidst or around a flagship series. Authors can take full advantage of the literary universe they've built by offering their readership a prequel series, which takes place before the events in the flagship story arc; or a spin-off series, which usually involves giving a secondary character from the anchor series their own story.

Examples of prequel series:

- *Fantastic Beasts and Where To Find Them* (film series)
- *The Hobbit* (film series)

Examples of spin-off series:

- The *Forgotten Gods* duology by Marie Rutkoski, a spin-off from *The Winner's Trilogy*
- *The Immortals* quartet by Tamora Pierce, a spin-off from the *Song of the Lioness* quartet
- *The Beatrice Letters* by Lemony Snicket, a spin-off from *A Series of Unfortunate Events* series
- *The Last Hours* series by Cassandra Clare, a spin-off from *The Mortal Instruments* series

Box set of series starters

One way you can lure readers into series set in the same literary universe is by bundling all of your series' first books into an omnibus or box set. This does entail you having at least three series out, but it's a great option for those looking to introduce their literary universe to a wider readership.

. . .

Sale of all series starters

Similarly, you could also run a sale on the individual first books of your series, creating graphics and copy that make it clear in your advertising that these books are an introduction to a whole literary world.

Social media and website graphics

Have your designer create a graphic that shows how all your series are linked and their possible reading order. There is a great example of this on Robin Hobb's website that shows her readers how to progress through her multi-series universe, *The Realm of the Elderlings*. It shows images of each of her series and how they fit alongside each other in an overall reading order. You can share graphics like this on your website and use them to promote your entire catalogue on social media or in your newsletters.

Author M.D. Cooper has gone one step further and set up an entire website devoted to the *Aeon 14 Universe*. The menu is easy to navigate, directing readers to book lists, where to start if they're new and how they can start reading for free.

Section VI: All the Rest

"As always, there are so many moving parts to this career and I find myself feeling a little lost today…"
(Author Diaries, August 10th, 2020)

TWENTY-FOUR

Combating Series Fatigue

"My enthusiasm for this new series (a quartet) comes in waves of varying sizes. One minute I'm completely elated, the next I feel utterly unoriginal and ordinary. The enormity of undertaking a quartet is not lost on me. A few times I've found myself contemplating this whole career path. To live, I'm going to have to be constantly creating (not to mention promoting), which at this point all feels a bit exhausting."
(Author Diaries, June 30th, 2019)

ONE THING we haven't addressed amidst all my calls for longer series, flagship series and staying in the same universe is the very real threat of *series fatigue*. You can imagine it, can't you? The exhaustion that not only comes with writing books, but that's specific to sticking with the same characters and settings for months or years on end...

At one time or another, we all experience this. Whether it's because of the series itself or life circumstances beyond our control, there will likely be a moment (or two) when an author just feels *done*; a moment where you'd rather take a big old nap rather than open up that series bible and hammer away at your keyboard. It's only human. But if you want to make a successful career from writing series (and to be fair, writing in general), it's something you'll have to learn to face and combat effectively.

1. A good offence is a good defence

Apparently I'm making sports analogies now, but this very much applies here. The best way to combat series fatigue is by being prepared for it from the beginning. This is where your market research, your planning and outlining, and everything else we discussed at the beginning of this book comes into play. Your passion for your genre will lead you back to your series in progress. If you've done all the relevant pre-production work, it will be much easier to combat series fatigue.

2. Take a break

Sometimes, when the writing isn't going well, it's not really about the writing. Sometimes, we authors just get tired. Burnt out. Zonked. It's not necessarily about our love for the world we've created or our story falling flat; it's about needing to rest and rejuvenate. This happens to the best of us, whether we're writing full-time or writing around a day job and family commitments. This career can be gruelling, and sometimes the only cure is to take some time off from writing. I have done this a handful of times when I've felt burnt out and overwhelmed. I know many of us struggle with the guilt of not writing, which is another beast in itself, but if you can manage to take a week away from your manuscript, it might be the breath of fresh air you need.

3. Take stock of your characters and plot

Sometimes, it *is* about the writing, but that doesn't mean it's the end of the world. Step back and take stock of your characters and plot. Have these fallen flat as you've been writing? Have you forgotten to layer in breadcrumbs and unanswered questions? Is there something you can do to create more intrigue surrounding your protagonist or antagonist? Try reading your work in progress on a different device to the one you write on. I like to send the manuscript to my Kindle or print it out and get away from my desk. Sometimes simply changing the format and setting of experiencing your work can shed much-needed light.

4. Revisit your outline (if you're an outliner)

If the very thought of your series is fatiguing you, perhaps the problem lies with the bigger picture. Despite how much we plan, sometimes things just don't work out the way we hoped, or a bolt of inspiration might take us in another direction. Revisit your outline: have you veered off course and created problems for yourself? Or alternatively, is your outline stifling your creativity? Both these things have happened to me at one point or another, and it always takes me a while to realise the reason I'm treading water is that my outline is no longer effective. There's nothing wrong with hitting pause on your current manuscript to rework your outline if needed. You might find that it reignites your passion for the series.

5. Talk to someone

Far too often, we authors sit alone all day, cooped up in our own heads. I often find that an honest conversation about my struggles or worries is an immense help. In articulating the problem, I often find the solution. Brainstorming with a trusted friend has also been an invaluable way to combat series fatigue. Someone else's enthusiasm can reignite your own.

6. Prioritise creative input

Often when we're feeling fatigued by the scope of our own series, it's because we're working ourselves into the ground without generating any creative energy. Ask yourself: when was the last time you read something for pleasure? Or binge-watched something utterly addictive with no guilt? When I allow myself the leisure time to unwind and enjoy the art of others, that's when the ideas come barrelling into me and that creative energy starts flowing again. If you don't have the energy or patience to start something new (this happens to me often), try revisiting your old favourites; reread a book you loved or rewatch a film or show you once raved about. You may find that these spark new ideas for your series.

7. Assess your team

On a handful of occasions that I felt serious series fatigue, I realised the issue wasn't with the writing itself, but some part of the production process. From personal experience I know that working with the wrong person can poison the way you feel about your work, particularly if this person has unconstructive views or their input isn't doing your hard work justice.

For me, this happened with a cover design once. The designer didn't answer my questions, took everything I said literally and didn't apply their own expertise to what would and wouldn't work, and ultimately I started to feel like their sloppy job was compromising the quality of the work I was publishing. I felt like I was fighting a losing battle to get the cover I had commissioned and eventually, this struggle seeped over into how I was feeling about the series as a whole. I had already commissioned the next cover in the series with this particular agency, but dreaded the experience. In the end I sent a firm email to the designer about the lack of communication and the quality of the service, suggesting that if things didn't improve I would take my substantial business elsewhere.

Every member of your team should make your job easier, not harder. There may come a time in your career where you need to re-evaluate who is on your team and make the tough decision to move on from a working relationship that's causing more harm than good.

TWENTY-FIVE

Managing Multiple Books and Multiple Series

"I'm juggling a lot at the moment and just want to GO, GO, GO... I might pause outlining for a moment to upload the With Dagger and Song *files to Ingram and reply to the designer re: Book 3 cover. Then, back to outlining, just realised I'm meant to start drafting next week!"* (Author Diaries, August 27th, 2021)

THERE WILL COME a time in your career where you'll be managing the production and promotion of multiple books in your series, and at some point, multiple series. This is no easy feat, and trust me when I say it takes some time to wrap your head around. For example, at the time of writing, I am:

- Preparing to launch book three in *Curse of the Cyren Queen*
- Managing the cover creation of book four
- Awaiting beta reader feedback on book four
- Writing and reworking this book you now hold in your hands

- Slowly researching and doing creative input for a new fiction series
- Continuing to promote *The Oremere Chronicles* and existing *Curse of the Cyren Queen* books

This is just with two (potentially three) series… Imagine what it's going to look like when there are more series and titles in my backlist. It has the potential to cause serious overwhelm (and has done so on numerous occasions).

Writing and publishing series takes organisation, patience and a variety of tools to stay on top of the various stages of production, promotion and ideation. But what if you've only written a few books? What if your first series isn't complete? What if you haven't even put pen to paper on your first series starter yet? Am I jumping the gun by talking about managing multiple books and series?

Honestly? No. The sooner you work out your systems for managing multiple production lines, the better. It's far easier to trial certain systems when you don't have a huge back catalogue and you're not having to move masses of data around. It's also far more beneficial to you as an author to ingrain good organisational habits from the beginning so that when you become more prolific, the learning curve isn't as steep.

Have I convinced you yet? Good. Let's get stuck into the tools I use to manage multiple books and series…

Asset master list

I first came across the term "asset master list" in Joanna Penn's book *Your Author Business Plan: Take Your Author Career to the Next Level,* and I've kept one ever since. This is as simple as it sounds: it's a working list (mine is a spreadsheet) of my intellectual property assets, i.e. my books and their various formats, publication platforms and subsidiary rights. There is a column for each of the following:

- Title
- Language
- Audio rights situation (if the rights are sold and the term)
- Kindle
- KDP (Kindle Direct Publishing) print
- Ingram print
- Hardback
- Audiobook published
- Foreign rights print
- Translator/Rights
- Workbook
- Large print
- Apple Books
- Kobo

Not all of these columns are relevant to each of my titles – for example, as I'm enrolled in Kindle Unlimited for both of my fiction series, the columns for Apple Books and Kobo have been left blank, but when *this* book is added to the asset master list, it will have the other platforms marked as complete.

Foreign rights are a work in progress at the moment, so they're also left blank. Audio rights have been sold for all of my fiction titles for a term of seven years and have been marked accordingly. *The Oremere Chronicles* titles don't have "Ingram print" or "Hardback" checked off – when these were published, I used Amazon's expanded distribution through CreateSpace (the old print option for Amazon). This is something I intend to rectify in the near future and this list serves as a reminder of that task on my to-do list.

My asset master list is where I view my production at the highest level; where I can see what has been released and on what platforms, which rights have been sold and which are still up for grabs.

If you're planning on a long-term career as an indie author, I strongly advise you create something similar to keep track of your titles and subsidiary rights. I have a regular reminder in my calendar to update my asset master list. This makes managing multiple books across multiple series a little easier.

But what about managing your series on a more granular level? Let's get to that now.

Table of ongoing production

The next tool on my list is a table that allows me to see, at a glance, where each of my titles are in the various stages of production. The top row of the table lists the most important stages of my production process:

- Creative input (planning/research)
- Outline
- Draft #1
- Structural edit
- Beta feedback (round #1)
- Rework
- Beta feedback (round #2)
- Finalise manuscript
- Copyedit
- Proofread
- Cover finalised
- Approval of print copies
- Publication

ONGOING PRODUCTION

Book	C/I	O/L	D1	Str	B1	R/W	B2	Fin	CE	PR	C	App	Pub
ALOB	▨	▨	▨	▨	▨	▨	▨	▨	▨	▨	▨	▨	▨
WDAS	▨	▨	▨	▨	▨	▨	▨	▨	▨	▨	▨	▨	▨
TFOC	▨	▨	▨	▨	▨	▨	▨	▨	▨	▨	▨	▨	
TWAC	▨	▨	▨	▨	▨								
NF	▨	▨	▨	▨	▨	▨							
NS 1	▨												

The first column of the table lists an abbreviation for the title of each book: *A Lair of Bones, With Dagger and Song, The Fabric of Chaos, To Wield a Crown,* NF (nonfiction, i.e. this book right here) and then NS for "New Series", which will be my next major fiction project. I'm at various stages of production for all of them. When one of these stages is complete, I simply colour the box in for the relevant book.

Though it may seem basic, this little table (which admittedly is hand-drawn and Blu-Tacked to my wall) really helps me get a big-picture view of where all my titles are in the production line, and more importantly, what I should be focusing on currently.

As I mentioned earlier, when your manuscript is out of your hands, you should be focusing on the next one. This table tells me where I should be prioritising my words.

I've created a template for this table for you to access and use yourself at the back of this book. You may have different stages of production, so you could also use it as a starting point for creating your own.

Organisational tools

One thing I could no longer get by without is my calendar. I use Google Calendar for practically everything under the sun and colour-code the following categories:

- Book production tasks and deadlines
- Outreach campaigns (seeking reviews and content marketing opportunities)
- Paid marketing (booking promotions and running deals)
- Finance
- Newsletter content
- Social media
- Personal (like family birthdays, dinner reservations, etc. – they're easy to forget when you're this deep into writing and publishing series)

The tasks I add can be as small as "Add *The Fabric of Chaos* blurb to Goodreads" or as crucial as "Upload manuscript to KDP", but they are all colour-coded and specific, often containing detailed instructions in the description or links to the correct page. There are numerous tasks like this per book within each series; there are also multiple tasks for each overall series, like "Create box set" or "Run stacked series promotion"… And that's why it is *vital* that you find an organisational tool that works for you.

One thing I love about Google Calendar is the functionality to add recurring tasks. So for example, I try to apply for a BookBub Featured Deal once a month – I add this and set it to "Repeat Monthly", so I get a reminder and it's one less thing I have to remember. I do the same for my monthly finances, following up invoices and a variety of other tasks.

Whatever tool you choose to use, be it a digital calendar or a physical diary, I cannot stress enough the importance of writing things down and documenting your deadlines. There is such a huge learning curve with writing and publishing series that you can't possibly remember every single detail. You need to create an organisation system that works for you and your process.

Digitally filing the actual books

What about your actual manuscripts? At any given time you might have an outline on the go, a first draft of book three, a copyedited manuscript of book two and the proofed pages for book one... How do you keep track of them all?

I have several filing systems, none of which are incredibly sophisticated, but all of which do the job for me. My first port of call is Google Drive, where I have a folder called Books. Within this, I have folders for Fiction and Nonfiction. Within *these* folders, I have folders for each series – so for example, in my Fiction folder I have the following subfolders:

- *The Oremere Chronicles*
- *Curse of the Cyren Queen*
- *Next Series* (yep, that's all it's called at the moment)
- *Next Next Series* (I told you it wasn't sophisticated)

Within each of these are folders for each book in the series, so *The Oremere Chronicles* contains folders for *Heart of Mist, Reign of*

Mist, *War of Mist*, *Dawn of Mist* and Omnibus. Each of these contains the following folders:

- Back and front matter
- Beta reader materials
- Cover
- Outreach
- Planning
- Promotion
- Writing
- Other (for miscellaneous items)

The files in these folders are backed up onto my computer, and on a regular basis I back it all up again on a hard drive.

Over the years I've also learned to use the same naming convention for all my files to avoid the dreaded "Book-1-final-final-final" file. It looks like this: *BookTitle-Draft1-Date*. My print-ready files are titled *BookTitle-Paperback-V1* and so forth.

TWENTY-SIX

Mistakes Made and Lessons Learned

"... if you are making mistakes, then you are making new things, trying new things, learning, living, pushing yourself, changing yourself, changing your world. You're doing things you've never done before, and more importantly, you're Doing Something."
—Neil Gaiman, "My New Year Wish"

THERE IS no doubt in my mind that like me, *you will make mistakes* (likely many) when writing your own series – as you should. Mistakes are how we learn, how we better ourselves and our craft, and ultimately, how we improve the experience for our readers, which should always be the end goal. However, I hope that by sharing the following mistakes and lessons learned, I can save you from making the same ones as me.

So, without further ado, let's take a deep dive into the somewhat painful failings of my past self, as well as some of the common mistakes I've seen other authors make when writing series...

1. Not keeping a series bible for *The Oremere Chronicles*

I know, I know, I've already touched on this in the extensive chapter on series bibles. However, I want to emphasise how much unnecessary stress this caused me while I was writing the later books in the series, as well as how much stress it *will* cause if I ever choose to return to that story arc. Even as I write this, I have no point of reference or important details noted down for the majority of the characters and storylines that occurred throughout a three-book series (plus a prequel collection), which overall spans nearly half a million published words. Are you seeing the scope of this mistake yet?

I have distant plans to return to *Oremere* after my next series, in which I *may* unite several key players from each of my series. In order to do this accurately, I'll now need to spend weeks reading through *The Oremere Chronicles* and creating a series bible from scratch, which is a huge undertaking at this point. Had I simply created a working document from the beginning, I would have saved myself time during the writing process, but also time and energy years later when returning to those characters.

2. Not planning *The Oremere Chronicles*

In a similar vein: for the type of writer I am, not planning and outlining *The Oremere Chronicles* was a big oversight on my part. It was my first-ever series, so I can't be too hard on myself, but I learned the value of planning and outlining quite quickly as I started work on the later books and realised that the foreshadowing I needed hadn't been woven through. It took *many* hours of problem-solving with my beta readers to remedy such mistakes, which made my overall writing process twice as long and twice as painful. It's a mistake I won't make again.

3. Making story choices without a clear-cut reason

Something I've noticed I do is make firm decisions about the story (about a particular group of characters or setting, for example) without having a real reason to do so. It's only later when I come back to address something else that I realise I've written myself into a bit of a corner.

For example, originally in *Curse of the Cyren Queen*, I established the rule that no song played twice in the lair of bones. I wove this throughout the whole book, until during rewrites I realised that there was no legitimate reason for this to be the case and in fact, it made other elements of the story unrealistic. I had unintentionally made that aspect of the world unnecessarily complicated. In the end, I cut it out altogether.

Of course, these instances can't be avoided entirely – you're bound to make some sort of decision that will have an unknown consequence in later books. However, I've learned to interrogate my decisions on a deeper level at the beginning of the process to help narrow the chances of this happening.

4. Being too specific with timelines

This is a mistake I've made a few times and one I've seen many other authors make at the start of their series. Often when you define a certain timeline (e.g. saying something happened 900 years ago or in 1956), you're locking yourself in where you don't need to. Particularly earlier on in series, you can get away with being a little more vague in your references to time (unless you're writing historical fiction).

One way I've found around this is by referencing eras or ages without specifying the exact year it happened. For example, in *Curse of the Cyren Queen*, instead of saying "954 years ago", I refer to the Age of Chaos, which readers know to mean sometime in the distant past. I don't need to specify exactly how many years ago this occurred, and that prevents me from committing to an exact timeline of historic events that might come back to haunt me further down the track.

5. The tendency to put every idea into your first series

When you're starting your first series, there's a massive temptation to fill it with every great idea you've ever had (and maybe even some not-so-great ideas). Believe me, I've done the same thing. We get so overexcited and dead keen on making our series the biggest and best it can be that we forget to pause and consider the fact that we're going to be writing books for a long time yet. Not every idea we have may suit this particular series or that particular story arc, and it doesn't need to. We don't need to jam-pack all our ideas into one series, since ideally we'll be writing multiple more in the years ahead. Pick and choose from your ideas, save some for later, dismiss some altogether. Trust me – more will come.

6. Falling prey to middle/second book syndrome

Middle book syndrome is generally when an author's second or middle book doesn't quite live up to the quality of the previous book/s. In fact, you're probably more familiar with occurrences in the film industry. How often have you walked out of the cinema thinking, "That just wasn't as good as the first movie"? More than once, I'll wager.

Thankfully, this hasn't happened to me in a long while, but it has once before. Long before I started planning, one of my beta readers rightly told me that one of my earlier books was suffering from this syndrome. Essentially, it didn't have a story arc of its own and couldn't stand on its own two feet outside of the series arc. I remedied this in the structural editing stage, but it wasn't fun, which is why I advocate so much for thorough series planning: to avoid this problem from the outset. Since then, I've made sure that every one of my books has its own arc as well as being part of a series arc.

7. Losing sight of the joy of writing

At one point or another, you'll face series fatigue or one of the various other mental tolls of being a writer. When this happens, you might lose sight of the actual joy of writing. I know I certainly have on more than one occasion. Just take a look at this entry from my journal: "After yesterday's entry, I sat and tried to free write for the next prequel. Though I didn't write much, it felt good. I always forget that I should maintain some sort of writing even when I'm not in the midst of drafting. While I write in here regularly, and it's good for me, it's not the same as 'creating'. Whereas for that brief pocket of time yesterday when I put pen to paper and wrote about Deelie in Lochloria, I felt content." (Author Diaries, April 23rd, 2020)

And this one:

Don't lose sight of the joy of writing: I've taken the pressure off myself – no timers, light to-do lists and the permission to dismiss other tasks if the ideas are flowing. Why do I always have to learn this lesson the hard way? Once again, I got caught up in the idea of "production" and producing words. I certainly don't think I'm a romantic when it comes to the "artistic" side of being an author, but there's definitely merit in honouring the process. Part of my process is this initial stage: brainstorming on the whiteboards, using Post-it Notes, spreadsheets, lists, scribbling down random scenes to be slotted in later. I think I got swept up in the business side, in the need for more products without acknowledging that my brand of product needs this incubation period. That I'm allowed to revel in this process just a little.

(Author Diaries, August 27th, 2021)

If you're feeling fatigued, sometimes you need to take a step back and write something else, even if it's just for yourself, to cultivate new creativity and find the joy of writing again.

7. Genre- and series-hopping

This is a mistake I haven't made myself (only because I can't focus on more than one thing at a time), but I've heard many authors talk about how they genre-hopped too soon, or started writing a new series amidst an incomplete one. Ultimately, both these choices split your focus, efforts and time, meaning it'll take longer for any one series to be complete. Genre-hopping basically doubles the amount of work you need to do in terms of building an audience, and series-hopping can frustrate readers who have been patiently waiting for the next instalment of their favourite series. Neither are good things.

8. Not managing my expectations across multiple series

Another mistake I made in between the last *Oremere* book and the release of a new series starter was not managing my expectations. For whatever reason, I expected *Curse of the Cyren Queen* to sell in exactly the same way as my first series had. This was not the case. There was an array of influencing factors that I didn't take into consideration, such as:

- It would be two years between the release of *War of Mist* and *A Lair of Bones*, rather than my previous annual publication schedule
- A prequel collection and an omnibus (published in the year between) didn't bring in the same revenue as a full-length novel
- A global pandemic hit
- I used a different pricing strategy
- A new series starter is harder to sell than a sequel in an existing series

And that's just the tip of the iceberg. Since then, I've learned to adapt my expectations to the current circumstances and the state of the market. It has meant far less disappointment and stress. No matter how many series you write, they will not all experience the same level of success; however, the important takeaway here is that you're working towards a powerful backlist and a body of work that will eventually carry your career into the long term.

TWENTY-SEVEN

Commonly Asked Questions About Writing a Series

"What an author doesn't know could fill a book."
— Holly Black, *Lucinda's Secret*

OVER THE COURSE of researching and writing this book, I reached out to several indie author communities and asked what they struggled with and what they wanted to know the most about writing series. The following are the most common questions I received...

How should I title my series?

Depending on your publishing strategy, knowing your titles ahead of time could prove vital to your production schedule. In the past, titles were always something I decided on *after* the manuscripts were complete. However, two series in, with plans for a long and successful career ahead of me, I've started to understand the value in deciding these details in advance – as early as the outlining stage, if at all possible. But how do you decide on your series title and the titles of its individual books so that it's obvious they're in a series?

Here are some examples of series naming conventions:

- Using a character name: e.g. *Harry Potter and the Philosopher's Stone*, *Harry Potter and the* Chamber of Secrets etc. and *Percy Jackson and the* Lightning Thief, *Percy Jackson and the* Sea of Monsters etc.
- Named after the first book in the series: e.g. *A Court of Thorns and Roses*, *Throne of Glass*, *The Obernewtyn Chronicles*
- Named after a group of people within the series: e.g. *The Farseer Trilogy*, *The Black Dagger Brotherhood*, *Bridgertons*
- Named after a place: e.g. *The Oremere Chronicles*, *The Chronicles of Narnia*

As you can see, there are numerous ways to name both your series and the books within it. Consider the following tips:

- Choose something that's easy to say and remember (so readers can easily Google it when they hear it mentioned)
- Avoid weird spellings where possible (between my surname and the word "Oremere", readers were certainly challenged to find me)
- Remember that the series title will be the smaller title on the cover of your books
- Go back to your initial research – what are some of the popular series titles in your genre? Is there a

pattern used? Can you use this as inspiration for your own?

The individual book titles within your series also have immense branding power and the ability to bring all the books together by…

- Using a recurring word pattern or theme: e.g. *Heart of Mist, Reign of Mist, War of Mist*; *Dark Lover, Lover Eternal, Lover Awakened*; *Assassin's Apprentice, Royal Assassin, Assassin's Quest*
- Using the same number and structure of words: e.g. *A Lair of Bones, With Dagger and Song, The Fabric of Chaos, To Wield a Crown*
- Using a matching naming convention: e.g. *A Court of Thorns and Roses, A Court of Mist and Fury, A Court of Wings and Ruin*

Final titling tips

- Once you've chosen a pattern, stick to it throughout the series – consistency is key
- Consider how your titles fit and look on your covers (I had to change my original title for book three in *Curse of the Cyren Queen* because it didn't match the spacing of the previous covers)
- Don't commit to a title pattern that will be too rigid/restricting if you choose to extend your series or if your series takes you in an unexpected direction

Should I stockpile my series before releasing?

There are certainly benefits to stockpiling, i.e. writing at least the first two or three books in your series before releasing the first book. However, you do need to keep in mind the upfront costs of doing so. There will be editors, cover designers and proofreaders to pay, none of which come cheap if you're doing this properly. This can be hard on the bank account, and all the while you don't know if your series is going to sell or not.

Personally, I found having the first two books done before the series launch alleviated some of the pressure to produce on a tight deadline, as well as helping me layer in more foreshadowing and consistent story arcs throughout multiple books. However, I wouldn't recommend stockpiling an entire series before you release, as there's the risk that all that investment of time and money may not earn itself back.

How far in advance should I confirm my titles and get my covers?

Again, this can be a matter of personal preference. For both my previous series, I only knew the title of each book once I had finished the manuscript, which meant I couldn't have the cover designed until after the fact. This meant that I missed out on the discounts of bulk-buying covers that some designers and agencies offer. It also meant that sometimes the work on the covers felt disjointed. Moving forward, brainstorming the titles at the initial series planning stage will be my goal. This will mean being able to weave subtle nods to the title throughout each book as well as the overall series. It may also mean being able to take advantage of the above mentioned cover design discounts (and when you're writing in longer series, these can make a huge difference to your overall budget).

Is there a maximum number of books that draws in readers before they're put off by the length of the series?

This question is specific to genre. In fantasy and sci-fi, for example, readers are used to longer series, while readers of literary fiction are likely not. However, it's really all about how the author markets the series and communicates with their audience. If it's romance and the books are interconnected standalones, the author needs to make this clear so their potential readers aren't overwhelmed by a 20-book series. It's also important that an author communicates with their audience about the expected series length.

For both my previous series, I stated from the beginning that one was a trilogy and one was a quartet, along with an estimate of my release schedule. Readers will appreciate your transparency and honesty, even if it's along the lines of, "I expect this series will run for six to nine books, but I don't know for sure yet; it depends on what the story requires." For the most part, I've found that readers are incredibly understanding and patient when an author takes the time to communicate with them.

Map FAQs

A big topic of conversation and confusion that came up time and time again was maps. How can an author use maps in their series? How to draft them? Who to contact to make one? Do you include a map in every book or just the first in the series? Let's break these down…

How can an author use maps in series?

One way I've used maps to my advantage is by linking settings across various series. As I explained earlier, the map from

The Oremere Chronicles can actually be matched up with the map from *Curse of the Cyren Queen*, showing that they're set in the same overall realm.

Within a single series, you can use a map to leave breadcrumbs for your reader. For example, the map for *The Oremere Chronicles* was originally partly shrouded in mist, but as we progressed through the series, more of the map was revealed with each book. The *Oremere* maps are also used to hint to the reader where the characters might travel.

Maps don't always need to span the immense continents that often feature in fantasy novels. They can serve a much simpler purpose of providing the reader with a reference point for a particular small town or city. It's completely up to the author how in-depth a map should be, or if one is needed at all.

Do I include my map in every book in the series?

Absolutely. A map is an asset that you've paid for that will be relevant throughout your whole series. Why would you make the readers who are up to book four flip back to book one to see the map? There's no issue with including the same map in each book as a reference point.

I'll give you an extra pro tip that may seem obvious: when designing your map, make sure that it's applicable to the whole series and doesn't need updating with each book to show more of the world. I learned quickly that having a new map designed for every book in the series gets very expensive. Have a single map designed that will serve you for the entire series if you can.

What are the best programs or tools for writing a series?

Ultimately, the only thing you need to write a series is a computer. Everything else is just icing on the cake. Again, the tools and programs you use are entirely dependent on what suits your individual process and methods. Most authors I know swear by the novel-writing software Scrivener, but for where I'm at right now, I prefer the simplicity of Google Docs and Microsoft Word – that's just a personal choice. I also like to start my initial series planning on three big whiteboards in my office and jot ideas down in a notepad, whereas a lot of my author friends swear by Notion and/or mind-mapping software.

There are no "best" tools, only the best tools for *you*. It's up to you to experiment with a variety of methods and programs to work out what suits you and your process. But so I'm not leaving you hanging, here are a few places to start:

- Notepad/pen
- Microsoft Word or Google Docs
- Scrivener
- Whiteboards
- Notion
- Asana
- Spreadsheets
- Post-it Notes on a wall

Ultimately it doesn't matter what you use to write, as long as you write.

How many words should I aim for in each book?

Again, this is entirely dependent on the genre of your series. Go back to the planning and research stage. What is the average length of the bestsellers in your genre? Start there.

How do I work out how big my series should be (e.g. two big books versus four smaller books)?

Revisit your comp titles and see what the bestsellers in your genre are doing. While it can be tempting to split larger books into multiple smaller ones, there's no point if these shorter books are going to upset reader expectations and earn you bad reviews. Within each genre there are expectations when it comes to book length that can't be ignored. For example, an epic fantasy series will likely contain several books that are each over 100,000 words, whereas a romance series of interconnected standalones might warrant an individual book length of, say, 60,000 to 80,000 words. This is where your research is incredibly important.

Should I finish every series I start?

Yes. Even if you have to wrap up a series prematurely because the sales are tanking, I'd never advise that you simply cease writing the series without an ending. All this is doing is showing readers that you can't be trusted to finish a story. Why would they ever invest in one of your books again? It damages your reputation and ultimately lets down those who have loyally stuck by you through the first few books. This is where exit and expansion strategies come into play. If you've planned properly, you should already have an escape route if things aren't going well. It's much better than disappointing your readers and risking them feeling spurned by your books.

How much should I read in my genre before starting my series? Should I focus on traditional or indie books?

Ideally, you should be writing in a genre you love reading, and therefore you should have read dozens, if not 100+ books in your genre before writing your series. You should be aware of reader expectations in terms of genre tropes, book length and story structure from the very beginning. And don't stop reading once you start writing – your education in your genre should be ongoing.

Personally, I never focused on how the books I read were published in terms of traditional versus indie, and in all likelihood, neither will your readers. They don't care if the logo on the spine says Penguin Random House or Tor, only that the story is compelling. Read extensively and widely, whether the titles are indie or trad (ideally both).

Should I spend any time looking at reviews for a book earlier in the series and adjust based on these (e.g. spend more time on characters readers are loving)?

This depends on how far into the series you've already written before publishing. If there is room for adjustments (i.e. the copyedit hasn't been completed), I would definitely consider tweaking the content to reward those readers who are not only enjoying the books but taking the time to leave reviews as well. However, for the most part, I'm already quite far into the series when early reviews come in, and more often than not, the characters the readers are enjoying are the ones I had planned for anyway, based on the research I had done.

Should I focus on certain tropes across a whole series and different tropes for each individual book?

Tropes are an interesting topic, as they can be as large as spanning a whole series, or small enough to only warrant a scene. For example, an epic quest can span several books, whereas the "only one bed" trope (where there's only one bed for two characters to share) can really only be stretched to a scene or chapter at most.

Throughout my research and planning stage, I brainstorm numerous tropes to include on both levels. For example, "enemies to lovers" might span the whole series, while "trapped in a blizzard" may only last one chapter. I approach tropes in a layered way – creating a list of those I feel best suit my genre and story arc and then weaving them throughout both the individual books and the series as a whole.

If I'm a slower writer, are there marketing tactics I can use to keep readers excited for the next book?

Absolutely – though I'll keep my suggestions brief, because "marketing a series" is a topic for another book entirely.

We already explored my preferred method for this in the chapter on reader magnets. This is the tactic I used when I was only publishing one book a year. In order to keep my readers invested in the series despite the long wait between books, I sent prequel short stories to my mailing list to keep their appetites hungry. All up, I sent nine short stories, three between each book, each focusing on one of the point-of-view characters from the main series. Your mailing list is the key to keeping your readers invested between books. You can keep them keen by sending short stories, behind-the-scenes snippets of your author life, deleted scenes, teaser quotes for the upcoming book, cover reveals and excerpts, and so on.

How successful are series that grow with the reader, e.g. a few in YA and then branching into new adult or adult, or middle grade to YA like *Harry Potter*?

This is an incredibly hard thing to measure and there will always be outliers in every genre. If this is something you're hoping to do in your series, my best advice is to find series similar to yours in the same genre and see how they're doing chart-wise and review-wise. Again, this is where doing your research can inform the entire direction of your series.

How big should my cast be?

The answer to this question will be entirely unique to your series. However, my rule of thumb is that it should be big enough to sustain multiple books and create interesting dynamics between your characters, but not so big that the reader can't connect with the main players.

Conclusion

This book went through many iterations throughout 2021, but the angle for this final version came to me at a very relevant time in the early weeks of 2022. I was in the process of wrapping up my second fiction series and looking ahead to what might come next. I knew it had to be a fantasy series, one that built upon the best of what I'd already done and the lessons I'd learned over the years. I found that this gave me the unique position of being able to study and deconstruct the concept of writing a series from the ground up, in real time.

Using a combination of my own experiences and endless hours of research, I developed a deeper understanding and fascination for the subject, and I hope that in joining me for the ride, you have come to appreciate the power of writing in series just as I have.

I realise there's a lot of information here to be processed, mulled over or debated, but whatever type of writer you are, I hope this book has given you a solid starting point for how to approach your own series. I truly believe this can lay the foundation for a long-lasting career as an indie author.

Writing this book has been an incredibly rewarding process, and as ideas for a brand-new fantasy series start to snowball in my mind, I continue to realise just how intricate the world of series writing can be. But of course, writing is only *part* of the journey... As indies, *publishing and marketing* are our business as well. Hint, hint.

If there's one thing I've come to appreciate about this career, it's that there's no limit to learning. The more books and series you write, the more deeply you'll understand their impact in terms of your own long-term success.

So, what are you waiting for? It's time to get writing.

References

I've referred to a lot of books, TV shows, films, articles and blog posts throughout this book.

You'll find them all listed below. You can also download this with clickable links, as well as the recommended resources here: www.helenscheuerer.com/write-successful-series-resources

Aaron, Rachel. 2017. *2K to 10K: Writing Faster, Writing Better, and Writing More of What You Love*. Published independently.

Altair, Zara. 2019. "Supercharge Your Author Career with a Series." Prowritingaid.com. February 12, 2019. https://prowritingaid.com/art/842/-supercharge-your-author-career-with-a-series.aspx.

Atwood, Margaret. 1981. "Spelling" in *True Stories*. Toronto: Oxford University Press.

Bach, Richard. 1974. *A Gift of Wings*. New York: Dell.

Breaking Bad. 2013. Season 5, episode 16, "Felina." Directed by Vince Gilligan. Aired September 29, 2013, on AMC.

Bridgeport Herald. 1897. "At The Theatres." November 21, 1897. Google News Archive

Cannon, Sarra. 2018. "How to Write a Best-Selling Series (and What Is an Anchor Series?)" Heart Breathings. March 14, 2018. https://heartbreathings.com/how-to-write-a-bestselling-series/.

Cannon, Sarra. 2020. "How to Create a Series Bible (How to Plan & Write a Series, #4)". Heart Breathings. July 30, 2020. https://heartbreathings.com/how-to-create-a-series-bible-how-to-plan-write-a-series-4/.

Collins, Suzanne. 2008. *The Hunger Games.* New York, New York: Scholastic Inc.

Diterlizzi, Tony, and Holly Black. 2003. *The Spiderwick Chronicles: Lucinda's Secret.* New York: Simon & Schuster Books For Young Readers.

Estes, David. 2022. Email interview with Helen Scheuerer. David's website: http://davidestesbooks.blogspot.com/.

Faulkner, William. 1956. *The Paris Review.* Issue 12, Spring 1956.

Fayet, Ricardo. 2021. *How to Market a Book: Overperform in a Crowded Market (Reedsy Marketing Guides).* Published independently.

Forsyth, Kate. 2014. "Ghostwriting, Crime writing, tips from HarperCollins editors and bestselling author Kate Forsyth". So You Want to be a Writer. July 14, 2014.

Fox, Chris. 2015. *5,000 Words Per Hour: Write Faster, Write Smarter.* Chris Fox Writes LLC.

Fox, Chris. 2016. *Six Figure Author: Using Data to Sell Books.* Chris Fox Writes LLC.

Fox, Chris. 2016. *Write to Market: Deliver a Book that Sells.* Independently published.

Fox, Chris. 2019. "Flagship Series with Chris Fox" at Sell More Books Show Summit.

Gaiman, Neil. 2004. "Pens, Rules, Finishing Things and Why Stephin Merritt Is Not Grouchy." Neil Gaiman's Journal. May 2, 2004. https://journal.neilgaiman.com/2004/05/pens-rules-finishing-things-and-why.asp.

Gaiman, Neil. 2011. "My New Year Wish." Neil Gaiman's Journal. December 31, 2011. https://journal.neilgaiman.com/2011/12/my-new-year-wish.html.

Game of Thrones. 2014. Season 4, episode 8, "The Mountain and the Viper." Directed by Alex Graves. Aired June 1, 2014, on HBO.

Game of Thrones. 2017. Season 7, episode 1, "Dragonstone". Directed by Jeremy Podeswa. Aired July 16, 2017, on HBO.

Goins, Jeff. 2017. "Stop Trying to Be Famous and Build a Body of Work Instead." Jeff Goins. December 16, 2017. https://goinswriter.com/body-of-work/.

Hartinger, Brent. 2017. "Writing Sequels: 7 Rules for Writing Second Installments." Writer's Digest. December 3, 2017. https://www.writersdigest.com/write-better-fiction/7-rules-writing-sequels.

Hobb, Robin. 1995. *Assassin's Apprentice*. New York, New York: Del Rey.

Holiday, Ryan. 2015. "The Strategies That Helped Me Write 3 Books in 3 Years." Ryan Holiday. March 30, 2015. https://ryan-holiday.net/the-strategies-that-helped-me-write-3-books-in-3-years/

Hunt, Crystal. 2019. *Strategic Series Author: Plan, Write and Publish a Series to Maximize Readership & Income*. The Creative Academy.

Jackson, Peter, director. 2001. *The Fellowship of the Ring*. New Line Cinema.

Johnson, Elana M. 2021. *Writing and Launching a Bestseller*. AEJ Creative Works.

Johnson, Elana M. 2020. *Writing and Marketing Systems*. AEJ Creative Works.

King, Stephen. 2000. *On Writing*. London, England: Hodder & Stoughton.

King, Stephen. 2003. *The Gunslinger*. Viking Penguin.

Kristoff, Jay. 2018. *Godsgrave*. London, England: Harper Voyager.

Labrecque, Tammi L. 2018. *Newsletter Ninja: How to Become an Author Mailing List Expert*. Newsletter Ninja.

McLinn, Patricia. 2021. "Discovery Writing And Sustaining A Long-Term Writing Career With Patricia McLinn." The Creative Penn. May 24, 2021. https://www.thecreativepenn.com/2021/05/24/discovery-writing/.

Lucas, George, director. 2002. *Star Wars: Attack of the Clones (Episode II)*. 20th Century Studios.

Maas, Sarah J. 2018. *Throne of Glass*. New York: Bloomsbury.

Martelle, Craig. 2018. *Become a Successful Indie Author: Work Toward Your Writing Dream*. Craig Martelle Inc.

Martelle, Craig. 2019. *Pricing Strategies: Maximize your bottom line for long-term financial health*. Craig Martelle Inc.

Martin, George R.R. 2014. *A Dance with Dragons*. London: Harper Voyager.

MasterClass Staff. 2021. "Writing 101: Foreshadowing Definition, Examples of Foreshadowing, and How to Use Foreshadowing in Your Writing." MasterClass. August 25, 20201. https://www.masterclass.com/articles/what-is-foreshadowing-foreshadowing-literary-device-tips-and-examples#what-is-foreshadowing.

McKee, Robert. 2014. *Story: Substance, Structure, Style, and the Principles of Screenwriting*. London: Methuen.

Morris, Mary. 1990. "Margaret Atwood, The Art of Fiction No. 121." *The Paris Review,* Winter 1990. https://www.theparisreview.org/interviews/2262/the-art-of-fiction-no-121-margaret-atwood.

Penn, Joanna. 2016. *The Successful Author Mindset: A Handbook for Surviving the Writer's Journey.* Curl Up Press.

Pratchett, Terry in Hertz, Sue. 2016. *Write Choices: Elements of Nonfiction Storytelling.* CQ Press.

Puglisi, Becca, and Angela Ackerman. 2017. *The Emotional Wound Thesaurus: A Writer's Guide to Psychological Trauma.* JADD Publishing.

Rosett, Sara. 2020. *How to Write a Series: A Guide to Series Types and Structure plus Troubleshooting Tips and Marketing Tactics.* United States: McGuffin Ink.

Rothfuss, Patrick. 2007. *The Name of the Wind.* New York: DAW Books.

Rowling, J.K. 1997. *Harry Potter and the Philosopher's Stone.* Bloomsbury.

Rucker, Christa. 2004. "Keys to Great Endings." FM Writers. http://www.fmwriters.com/Visionback/Vision20/themekeyes.htm.

Sanderson, Brandon. 2009. "What Is the Cosmere®?" Brandon Sanderson. November 23, 2009. https://www.brandonsanderson.com/what-is-the-cosmere/.

Schwab, V.E. 2017. *A Conjuring of Light.* London: Titan Books.

Shannan, Krystal. 2022. Email interview with Helen Scheuerer. Krystal's website: https://www.krystalshannan.com/.

Stephenson, Nick. 2022. R*eader Magnets: Build Your Author Platform and Sell more Books on Kindle (2022 Edition)*. Your First 10,000 Readers.

Strawser, Jessica. 2010. "David Morrell & Ken Follett Talk About Writing." Writer's Digest. October 8, 2010. https://www.writers-digest.com/improve-my-writing/follett-morrell.

Weiland, K.M. 2013. *Structuring Your Novel: Essential Keys for Writing an Outstanding Story*. Scottsbluff, Nebraska: PenForASword Publishing.

Weiland, K.M. 2016. *Creating Character Arcs: The Masterful Author's Guide to Uniting Story Structure, Plot, and Character Development*. Scottsbluff, Nebraska: PenForASword Publishing.

Wendig, Chuck. 2018. "Why Writing A Series (Especially As A New Author) Is Really Goddamn Hard." Terrible Minds. August 27, 2018. https://terribleminds.com/ramble/2018/08/27/why-writing-a-series-especially-as-a-new-author-is-really-goddamn-hard/.

York, Zoe. 2019. *Romance Your Brand: Building a Marketable Genre Fiction Series*. ZoYo Press.

York, Zoe. 2020. *Romance Your Plan: Taking Genre Fiction Marketing to the Next Level*. ZoYo Press.

Recommended Resources

Tools

- OneNote: https://onenote.com
- Scrivener: https://literatureandlatte.com/scrivener
- Notion: https://notion.so
- Asana: https://asana.com

Marketing & Publishing

- Starting from Zero (David Gaughran's free course): https://courses.davidgaughran.com/courses/starting-from-zero
- K-lytics Market Reports: https://k-lytics.com
- Reedsy: https://reedsy.com
- Mark Dawson's Self Publishing Formula 101 Course: https://learn.selfpublishingformula.com/p/101
- *Your Author Business Plan: Take Your Author Career to the Next Level* by Joanna Penn

Story Templates/Formula/Outlining

- Derek Murphy's One-Page Novel Plot Outline (based on the three-act structure): https://creativindie.com/plot-outline
- *Save the Cat Writes a Novel* by Jessica Brody (has templates for a variety of genres)
- *Romancing the Beat: Story Structure for Romance Novels* by Gwen Hayes
- Plottr: https://plottr.com

Worldbuilding

- Brandson Sanderson's Laws of Magic: https://brandonsanderson.com/sandersons-first-law
- Fantasy worldbuilding questions: https://sfwa.org/2009/08/04/fantasy-worldbuilding-questions
- WorldAnvil: https://worldanvil.com
- Hiveword: https://hiveword.com
- Inkarnate (map designing tool): https://inkarnate.com

Favourite Writing Craft Resources

- Jenna Moreci's YouTube Channel
- *The Emotional Craft of Fiction: How to Write the Story Beneath the Surface* by Donald Maass
- Better Writers Series by Sacha Black
- *2k to 10k: Writing Faster, Writing Better, and Writing More of What You Love* by Rachel Aaron

- Now Novel blog: https://nownovel.com/blog
- Well Storied blog: https://well-storied.com/archive

Bonuses

Sign up to my mailing list to access my Successful Series Bonus Bundle which includes:

- My complete series bible for *Curse of the Cyren Queen*
- A full volume of my Author Diaries (referenced throughout this book)
- An extensive list of popular fiction series
- An ongoing production table template
- My word count tracker spreadsheet
- And more

In addition to the Successful Series Bonus Bundle, you'll also receive regular writing and publishing advice.

Sign up here: www.helenscheuerer.com/successful-series-bonus-bundle

Acknowledgements

This book is the product not only of the lessons I've learned myself, but of the lessons I've been taught by the numerous authors who came before me. As such, writing these acknowledgements feels like a bigger task than usual, but I'm going to give it my best shot...

First, thank you to Sacha Black: rebel queen, nonfiction mentor and voice memo life coach. Without you, I'm not sure this book would have come into being. Thank you for your encouragement, your incredible feedback and your ongoing support. Life would be dull and lonely without your angelic accent each morning. Thank you for the conversations that have undoubtedly made me a better author and businesswoman.

A special thank you to the wonderful David Estes and Krystal Shannan, who took the time to answer my questions and familiarise me with how a discovery writer might approach a series. I found your processes and insights so inspiring and I'm so grateful to you for having shared them with me.

Of course, a huge thank you to the authors who gave me permission to quote their wonderful work: Chris Fox (who asked to be referred to as "Lord Fox the Pompous"), Ricardo Fayet, Becca Puglisi and Angela Ackerman, Jessica Strawser, Brent Hartinger, Craig Martelle, Elana M Johnson, K.M. Weiland, Tammi L. Labrecque, Zoe York, Rachel Aaron, Sara Rosett, Crystal Hunt, Sarra Cannon, Derek Murphy, Joanna Penn and Nick Stephenson.

As always, thank you to my partner Gary Ditcher, who supported this detour into nonfiction wholeheartedly from the get-go. Your constant encouragement keeps me going during the darkest times.

To my editor and friend, Claire – thank you for your expertise, as well as the three-hour-long phone calls and endless understanding.

To my author friends, Jenna, Dan and Katlyn, our check-ins and chats make this job far less isolating. Thank you for being here for the ride and for inspiring me with all that you achieve.

To my fellow Aussie authors, Nattie and Chloe, thank you for sharing your feedback on the original outline for this book.

And last but never least, thank YOU, dear reader. I hope this book offered some insight into the world of series writing and that you learned something along the way that helps you get a few steps closer to your dream career.

About the Author

Helen B. Scheuerer is the fantasy author of the bestselling trilogy *The Oremere Chronicles* and the *Curse of the Cyren Queen* quartet. Her work has been highly praised for its strong, flawed female characters and its action-packed plots. More recently, she has also delved into publishing advice for authors with her debut nonfiction book, *How To Write A Successful Series*.

Helen's love of writing and books led her to pursue a Bachelor of Creative Writing at the University of Wollongong and a Master of Publishing at the University of Sydney. Now Helen lives amidst the mountains in Central Otago, New Zealand and writes full-time.

Learn more at:
www.helenscheuerer.com/for-authors

By the Same Author

Helen Scheuerer (fiction)

The Oremere Chronicles

Heart of Mist

Reign of Mist

War of Mist

Dawn of Mist

Curse of the Cyren Queen

A Lair of Bones

With Dagger and Song

The Fabric of Chaos

To Wield a Crown

Helen B. Scheuerer (nonfiction)

How To Write A Successful Series